Our Sisters' London

Feminist Walking Tours

Katherine Sturtevant

CHICAGO REVIEW PRESS

Library of Congress Cataloging-in-Publication Data

Sturtevant, Katherine.
    Our sisters' London : feminist walking tours / Katherine
Sturtevant. — 1st ed.
              p.   cm.
        ISBN 1-55652-079-4 : $11.95
        1. London (England)—Description—1981- —Tours.
    2. Feminism—England—London—History—Guide-books.
    3. Women—England—London—History—Guide-books.
    4. Walking—England—London—Guide-books.
    I. Title.
    DA679.S89   1990
    914.2104'858--dc20

Of the many people who helped to make this book possible I would like especially to thank Lee Sturtevant, Isabel Stuart, Ray Meurer, and the folks at QIC who provided a home for me while I was in London.

Photographs courtesy of The National Portrait Gallery, London.

Published by Chicago Review Press, Incorporated,
814 North Franklin Street, Chicago, Illinois, 60610

1 2 3 4 5 6 7 8 9 10
ISBN 1-55652-079-4
Printed in the United States of America

For my grandmother,
Leisa Bronson,
one of my favorite travellers

Contents

Introduction

"I must have London, combined with the sun, the moon and the stars, with land or with water, to fill my imagination and excite my contemplation," wrote novelist Elizabeth Inchbald in 1810. Countless women, resident and transient, have felt the same. London is and has always been stimulating: It makes you feel alive, alert, as though you are at the center of things.

The vast, multicultural, exciting London of today is deeply rooted in the raucous, burly London of yesterday. Today the sidewalks are crowded with postcard racks and souvenir stands; once they were filled with hawkers crying their wares. Today you would be wise to be on guard against pickpockets as you ride the tube or make your way through a crowd; once you would have been a mark for robbers and footpads as well. The sari shops and Arab groceries on Tottenham Court Road; the West Indian and African students, are the logical fruit of seeds planted centuries ago as England began to expand into Empire.

This book is for those who enjoy the thrill of the historical. It is for those who, standing in front of a house in which Virginia Woolf once lived, feel a little shivery as they think to themselves: "She once walked up those very steps with her very feet!" It is

1

also for people who want to know more about the women who have lived and worked in London. We've all heard of Queen Elizabeth and Anne Boleyn, but what about Elizabeth Godfrey, the silversmith, or Elizabeth Mallet, who started London's first daily newspaper in 1702? In these pages you'll meet over three hundred ordinary and extraordinary women: queens, writers, painters, prostitutes, actresses, craftswomen, runaway slaves, Jewish financiers, reformers, suffragettes. Were they feminist women? Some of them certainly were; many of them emphatically were not. The women I have included in this book are women who have captured my imagination. I have not hesitated to include, when they interested me, often told tales of queens and royal mistresses. I have included women of achievement such as writers, actresses, and reformers, some celebrated and some forgotten. Some of the women I mention have made their way into history by virtue of their wealth and nobility; some because of their eccentric ways and zest for living; a few because they were victims of an infamy worth remembering. I have paid special attention to the moments in women's lives that demonstrate such qualities as strength, rebellion against the status quo, or a loyalty toward their own sex. The women I have chosen were not all admirable women, but they were all interesting women.

The chronology of women in London begins with a confused scattering of names in the first century A.D.: a Roman slave, a rebellious Briton. The exploits of the Saxons and saints who dominated the centuries that followed were not centered in London, so by and large these fierce and fascinating women do not appear in the pages of *Our Sisters' London*. It is not until the Middle Ages that we hear again about the women of London, and we hear first, of course, of the queens. But before long the noble names are joined by humbler ones: tradeswomen whose activities are recorded in guild records; medieval Jewish women who are remembered either for the business deals they made or for the persecutions they suffered.

The position of women in England has varied tremendously over the centuries. Many people assume that the march of progress has meant a gradual movement for women from bondage to liberation, but it's not that simple. Women in medieval times seem to have frequently practiced crafts and trades later restricted to men. Elizabeth I, who was crowned in 1558, was given the scholarly education common among the noblewomen of her day. Queen Anne, who came to the throne in 1702, had a Renaissance lady's education, and studied sewing and embroidery at the expense of history, mathematics, law, and even spelling and grammar. (She was, however, given thorough training in religion.) But even in Queen Anne's day, as in every era, there were exceptions. While the queen was at her needlework other women were writing novels, acting in plays, and sketching botanical specimens—for money. Class, of course, has always had a tremendous effect upon the achievements and behavior of women, sometimes in surprising ways.

It was during the eighteenth century that women's history began to be more than a record of exceptions. Though it was not until the end of the century that Mary Wollstonecraft wrote her famous essay, *Vindication of the Rights of Woman,* several decades previously a group of women had joined together in pursuit of intellectual stimulation. The Bluestockings, as they were called, were well-to-do women who were tired of playing cards and gossiping. Instead they hosted and attended salons at which topics of intellectual and literary interest were discussed with lively enthusiasm. These women were serious about their studies and about their bonds with one another. Several very intense friendships existed among their network.

In the mid-nineteenth century women began getting tough about their rights. They grew tired of well-reasoned pamphlets which pleaded for educational opportunities for women. They were ready for that golden key: the Vote. Women attended meetings, signed petitions, and shocked Victorian sensibilities by speaking in public. At the same time, the drive to enter the professions was gathering strength. Women wanted to practice medicine and law on the same terms as men.

The struggle grew fierce in the early decades of the twentieth century, when the colorful militant suffragettes arrived on the scene. The Women's Social and Political Union, founded by Emmeline Pankhurst and run by herself and her daughter Christabel, performed acts of militancy that were sometimes shocking and divisive, and sometimes very creative. (On one occasion, some suffragettes carved up a golf course, incising slogans such as NO VOTES—NO GOLF. The editor of *Golfing* wrote in an aggrieved fashion that golfers were not, on the whole, very political. The suffragists replied: Maybe now they will be.) The exploits of these women pepper the pages of *Our Sisters' London* for the same reasons they repeatedly dominated the headlines of English newspapers. The militant suffragettes were daring, scandalous, preposterous, and outrageous. Nothing makes better reading. But the WSPU was not the only show in town, even in its day, and the activities of the breakaway Women's Freedom League and of the working-class East London Federation of the Suffragettes are also covered.

Though women from many centuries and walks of life appear in *Our Sisters' London*, in any work of limited scope much is necessarily left unsaid. Scores of women who have contributed to London's history have had to remain unnamed, and of any individual woman mentioned it has been possible to say only a very little. Furthermore, though I have had to limit my book to the districts of central London, the outskirts of the city are likewise rich with the history of our sex, and readers are urged to go further afield. By all means visit Kew Palace, where Fanny Burney was once Keeper of the Robes, or the Kensal Green cemetery, where that eccentric woman Dr. James Barry is laid to rest. The house where the illustrator Kate Greenaway once lived can be seen in Hampstead, and in Highgate Cemetery the bodies of such eminent and controversial writers as George Eliot, Christina Rossetti, and Radclyffe Hall lie moldering.

A Word About This Book

Whenever possible, I have used tube stations as the beginning and ending points for my walks. I've done this partly because the tube is the simplest and most convenient way to get around London (though not the most scenic), but chiefly because tube stations are well marked and easy to locate on London maps. Once you know where it is, you can arrive at the appropriate tube station by tube, bus, foot, or taxi.

London women really got around: That's why you'll see the *
symbol after the names of many women. This indicates that the
name appears more than once in the pages of *Our Sisters' London.*
Use the index to locate other references if you're interested in
finding out more about a particular woman.

The other symbol you'll see is a †. It will appear after the name
of a museum or other institution and indicates that information
about hours, admission fees, and access for those with dis-
abilities can be found in the appendix. (For the information of
those in wheelchairs I have noted the presence of stairs.)

Be forewarned: At any given time a certain percentage of
London is being restored or reconstructed, and no matter when
you take your trip something you want to see is bound to be
covered with scaffolding. In the same way, most museums rotate
their collections, and there is no guarantee that the particular
item you've come to see will be on display the day you've come
to see it. (If you desperately want to view a particular painting
or other item, by all means write in advance and arrange an
appointment. Most museums will be happy to accommodate
you if they can; you needn't be a scholar or an art historian.)
Such setbacks are a part of any journey; fortunately, there will
not be many of them. London has been watching the Thames roll
by for over two thousand years, and it will be there still, waiting
for you, when you arrive.

1

Bloomsbury

Begin and End: British Museum
(Nearest Tube Station: Tottenham Court Road
or Russell Square)

For a lot of feminist pilgrims to London the name Bloomsbury means Virginia Woolf, and indeed, that fascinating literary genius haunts many streets of the district. "I find Bloomsbury fierce and scornful and stony hearted, but . . . so adorably lovely that I look out of my window all day long," she wrote in a letter in 1924. Since that time Bloomsbury has changed, and the buildings of the University of London (which in 1878 became the first university in the United Kingdom to grant degrees to women on equal terms with men) now dominate much of the area. But the loveliness Woolf spoke of remains today, and even those who don't worship Woolf will enjoy walking through this fresh, green corner of London.

The true heart of Bloomsbury is the British Museum† on *Great Russell Street*. As you wander through the streets that surround it, you'll find yourself gazing in shop windows at used books, art prints, antiques, and stationery supplies, while every now and then a gleam of fruit or the familiar red shine of a Coca-Cola can draws attention to a grocer's shop. The museum itself is as dignified as any building in London, and that's saying a lot: Vast and classical, its pillars and pediment rise behind shiny black railings and guarded gateways. You may think you're getting a discouraging reception, but not at all. When the museum first opened at Montagu House in Great Russell Street, it was accessible only three hours a day, and then only to those who had made written application in advance. Today the labyrinthian treasure house has up to four million visitors a year and is a mecca for both tourists and scholars of many nationalities.

The huge and fascinating collections of the BM cannot be covered in a work of this scope, of course. But those interested in the history of goddess worship will want to have a look at the Romano-British statuettes representing such goddesses as Minerva, Luna, and Epona, the horse-goddess. The Egyptian galleries house intriguing items ranging from the mummy and coffin of an Egyptian priestess to a bronze cat wearing earrings, sacred to the goddess Bastet. And among the Greek antiquities you will find relics from the matriarchal Minoan civilization of ancient Crete.

Devotees of literature should not neglect the galleries of the British Library, which include handwritten manuscripts by **Charlotte Brontë*** (1816–1855), **Jane Austen*** (1775–1817), **George Eliot*** (1819–1880), and **Virginia Woolf*** (1882–1941). There is also a letter from **Marie Stopes*** (1880–1958) to Havelock Ellis. Still a virgin after five years of marriage, Stopes settled down to read every book on sex in the British Library, and went on to write *Married Love*, published in 1918 (the same year she married her second husband). It was probably the first sex manual to focus on women's pleasure.

In addition to housing relics, the British Museum is noteworthy because of the Bloomsbury Reading Room, a beautiful circular library with a high blue dome. The library has been frequented by a number of interesting women. The room was immortalized by **Virginia Woolf*** in her wonderful essay about women writers, *A Room of One's Own*: "The swing-doors swung open; and there one stood under the vast dome, as if one were a thought in the huge bald forehead which is so splendidly encircled by a band of famous names." The novelist **Dorothy Richardson** (1873–1957) used to spend all her spare time reading at the BM. She was at this time working as an assistant to a dentist in Harley Street. Richardson's novels—eventually published under the collective title *Pilgrimage*—helped to develop stream-of-consciousness technique. Another reader was the writer **Gertrude Stein*** (1874–1946), who in 1902 lived in nearby Bloomsbury Square with her brother Leo. Stein came to the library to read the novels of Trollope, in which she delighted, but neither Trollope nor her friendship with Bertrand Russell reconciled her to living in London, which she found too gray and grim for her taste. In 1903 she moved on to Paris, where she lived for the rest of her life with her lover, Alice B. Toklas, returning to her native United States only for visits and lecture tours. Stein wrote a variety of prose works, and her experiments with language outraged, amused, and influenced both literary circles and the larger public. (Use of the Reading Room is restricted to scholars, but if you stand near the swing-doors a few minutes before the hour, the guard will let you know when you can take a brief look around.)

Leave the BM by its main entrance and turn right into Great Russell Street, then right again into Bloomsbury Street, which, if you follow it north, will bring you to *Bedford Square*. The only complete Georgian square left in Bloomsbury, it was developed by the architect Thomas Laverton under the supervision of Lady **Gertrude Leveson-Gower** (d. 1794), widow of the fourth Duke of Bedford, in 1775. The square is charming, peaceful, and exclusive—the gardens are not open to the public. Four rows of dignified brick dwellings surround the central park, and each dwelling has wrought-iron balconies at the second-story windows and an archway of patterned brick around the door. The ornamental keystones in the archways are of Coade Stone, which was developed in the factory of **Eleanor Coade*** (d. 1796). Several of the interiors of the houses—most of which are now occupied by publishers or architectural firms—have ceilings painted by **Angelica Kauffmann*** (1741–1807), who worked in the decorative arts, designing Wedgewood china, ceilings, and mantlepieces, in addition to working on canvas.

One former resident of the square was **Agnes Strickland** (1796–1874), whose researches into the lives of the queens of England have provided a valuable starting point for later scholars. In 1849, the square was the site of the Bedford Ladies College, begun by **Elizabeth Jesser Reid** in an attempt to provide secular higher education for gentlewomen. The school was later moved to Regent's Park.

If you turn right into Montague Place and walk east, passing behind the British Museum, you'll come to *Russell Square*, the largest square in Bloomsbury and one of the largest in London. The generous square of green is diagonally divided into four parts by bench-lined walkways, and the shrubbery, together with the snack bar, make the square an appealing place to rest on nice mornings in spite of the zooming traffic nearby. Russell Square is now surrounded primarily by banks, businesses, and hotels, but once it was entirely residential. On the southeast side of the square, at No. 56, **Mary Russell Mitford** (1787–1855) once lived, and she gave a literary dinner party there in 1836 for Wordsworth and others. By this time she was already a successful dramatist, but she was even more celebrated for her sketches of village life, based on her own experiences in Three Mile Cross near Reading, where she lived with her parents almost all her life.

The **Pankhursts***, the famous suffragette family, lived at No. 8 Russell Square (now part of the Russell Hotel on the east side of the square), from 1888 to 1893. The sisters **Christabel***, **Sylvia***, and **Adela** used to play in the square as children. Adela Pankhurst (1885–1961) is the least famous of the sisters, but she, too, was active in the Women's Social and Political Union, which her mother founded. Like Sylvia, she had a disagreement with the WSPU over policy, and eventually she emigrated to Australia, where she worked in the pacifist and socialist movements. But her energies found different channels after the death of her husband, Tom Walsh. She became a nurse for retarded children, and she was received into the Roman Catholic church shortly before she died.

Russell Square was also the location of the women's suffrage office at which Mary Datchett, fictional character of **Virginia Woolf*** in the novel *Day and Night*, worked.

Leave Russell Square at its eastern corner and walk south on busy Southampton Row, and after a short distance you'll see a sign directing you to *Queen Square* by way of a footpath to the left (east). Smaller than Russell Square, Queen Square is also far quieter. On the south side of the square, at No. 43, is the **Mary Ward*** Centre, an adult education institution which offers a variety of courses and services to the public. The center is named after the nineteenth-century novelist and philanthropist better known as Mrs. Humphrey Ward (1851–1920). Although she opposed votes for women—she was the first president of the Anti-Suffrage League—Mary Ward defended women's right to higher education and was secretary of Somerville College at Oxford for a time. Her novel *Robert Elsmere*, which was viewed by many as an attack on Christianity, was highly controversial. "It really almost started a new religion," wrote Ward's contemporary, Janet Courtney. "Elsmerism, as a variant on agnosticism, a new form of humanism, became the fashionable creed of the day."

What is now the Mary Ward Centre was, from 1861 to 1908, the Female School of Design. The school, which had been operating in Gower Street, was nearly forced to close due to lack of funds, but an appeal for public support made in 1861 was successful, and the institution moved that year to Queen Square. It remained there until it joined with the Central School of Arts and Crafts in 1908. During the 1870s the fees were £5 per five-month term for full-time students, or £3 per month for a three-day week, plus an entrance fee of ten shillings to all classes.

The north end of the square is dominated by the buildings of the National Hospital, but in 1771–72, when the future novelist and Bluestocking **Fanny Burney*** (1752–1840) lived here with her father, the north end of the square was still open, and Burney wrote an eloquent description of the view she had of Hampstead and Highgate. Burney had been writing plays and stories since the age of ten, but her juvenilia does not survive. On her eighteenth birthday, a year before she moved to Queen Square, she burned all her writings in a burst of religious remorse. After

Fanny Burney

Fanny Burney left but before the buildings of the National Hospital were erected in the 1880s, the north end of the square became associated with several interesting artistic and intellectual women. The workshop of William Morris, the socialist poet and craftsman whose firm produced furniture, stained glass, tapestries, carpets, wallpaper, and textiles, was here. A number of women were part of this enterprise, most commonly involved in traditional women's crafts such as embroidery. It was through exploring the techniques of medieval embroidery that **Jane Mor-**

ris (nee Burden), William's wife, and her sister **Elizabeth Burden** began to work for Morris & Co. Jane also did wood engraving, as did **Georgiana Burne-Jones.** Elizabeth later taught at the Royal School of Art Needlework. **Kate Faulkner** and her sister **Lucy** painted tiles, did gesso work, and designed wallpaper. In 1878 Lucy Faulkner (later Lucy Orrinsmith) published *The Drawing Room, Its Decoration and Furniture.* **May Morris** (1862–1938), William's daughter, was trained by her father. In 1885, when she was twenty-three, she was put in charge of the entire embroidery department.

No. 29, now part of the National Hospital, was the site of the Working Women's College, founded in 1864 by **Elizabeth Malleson** (1828–1916) and **Barbara Bodichon*** (1827–1891). Bodichon has a long list of credits as a feminist activist: She collected signatures for the Married Women's Property Bill in 1856; cofounded the *Englishwoman's Journal,* the first magazine of the women's movement in England, in 1858; and in 1860 helped to found the Society for Promoting the Employment of Women. She also helped Emily Davies* establish the school at Hitchin which eventually became Girton College, the first women's college at Cambridge. It is less widely known that part of the funds used for its establishment came from the sale of her paintings, for Bodichon was also an artist. After her marriage in 1857 to a French doctor, Eugene Bodichon, she spent her winters with him in Algeria, and many of her landscapes have Algerian settings. (Unconventionally independent, she continued to spend summers in England, on her own.) In 1854 Dante Gabriel Rossetti referred to her as a woman who was "blessed with large rations of tin [money], fat, enthusiasm and golden hair, who thinks nothing of climbing up a mountain in breeches, or wading through a stream in none, in the sacred name of pigment."

Queen Square was built between 1708 and 1720 and named for Queen Anne*, but the statue in the middle of the green is believed to be of Queen **Charlotte*** (1744–1818), consort of George III.

Leave Queen Square by its northeast corner, turning right on Guilford Street and left at the first opportunity into Grenville Street. This will take you into *Brunswick Square,* mentioned in

Jane Austen's* *Emma*. Emma's sister Isabella speaks quite firmly to their anxious father about it, saying, "You must not confound us with London in general, my dear sir. The neighborhood of Brunswick Square is very different from all the rest. We are so very airy!" Whether or not you agree with Isabella, the green square in the shadow of the modern, mall-style Brunswick Shopping Centre is a pleasant place to rest your feet. (There are probably more pleasant places to rest your feet in Bloomsbury than in all the rest of London.) The square was also once the site of a four-story home shared by **Virginia Woolf***—then Virginia Stephen—with Duncan Grant, John Maynard Keynes, her brother Adrian, and her future husband Leonard Woolf. The household broke up when Leonard and Virginia married in 1912.

Continue past the square (you are now on Hunter Street) and turn right (east) into Handel Street. This will lead you to *St. George's Gardens*, a curious and charming park dotted with the tombs and headstones that once lay in the churchyard of St. George the Martyr, Queen Square. Among these—perhaps it is one of the many whose inscription has been erased by time and weather—must lie the stone for **Julia Betterton Glover*** (1779–1850), actress, who was buried there in 1850. Glover's career included many "breeches" parts, but her performance in the role of Falstaff was panned by the critics, even though she had one of the largest waistlines on the English stage. She was described as elegant, commanding, graceful, and energetic, and was the leading comic actress of her day. However, her face was considered too round for tragedy.

Leave the Gardens the way you arrived and turn right into Hunter Street, then left (west) into *Tavistock Place*. The building at No. 9 was once the Passmore Edwards Settlement, founded by **Mary Ward***. The hall offered lectures, concerts, and clubs in its effort to serve as a social center for women and men in all walks of life. It was here that **Millicent Fawcett*** (1847–1929) and Ward debated the question of women's suffrage in February of 1909. When the discussion was over, the audience voted 235 to 74 in favor of women's suffrage, a result that surprised and displeased Mrs. Humphrey Ward. "I shall *never* do this sort of thing again, *never*," she told Fawcett backstage, "and I shall write to the papers to say so." Later she claimed that the meeting had been deliberately packed with Fawcett's supporters.

Tavistock Place will lead you to another bit of Bloomsbury greenery, *Tavistock Square*. No. 52, one of several addresses occupied by the novelist **Virginia Woolf*** (1882–1941), once stood on the southeast side of the square, where the Tavistock Hotel is now. The apartments of Virginia and her husband, Leonard Woolf, were in a typical nineteenth-century block of dark brick, with a railing about the basement windows. Woolf did her writing in a large room with a skylight, previously a billiard room, which she called the Studio. The light, spacious rooms were decorated by Woolf's sister, the painter **Vanessa Bell*** (1879–1961) and by Duncan Grant. The basement housed the Hogarth Press, on which the Woolfs printed—in addition to works by Virginia and Leonard—poems by T. S. Eliot, and the short story "Prelude" by the remarkable writer from New Zealand, **Katherine Mansfield*** (1888–1923).

The Woolfs moved to No. 52 in March of 1924, and it remained their London home for fifteen years. During this time Virginia produced her innovative masterworks *To the Lighthouse* and *The Waves*. They moved their things out just nineteen months before Woolf drowned herself in the River Ouse.

In the southeast corner of the green is a double-sided monument to Dame **Louisa Aldrich-Blake** (1865–1925). It can be viewed from the sidewalk, against a leafy backdrop of shrubbery, or from within the park itself. Either view shows the same bronze bust, on a pillar rising from a circular stone seat in the corner of the park. This tough-looking woman was the first woman in the country to gain the degree of Master of Surgery. She was Dean of the London School of Medicine for Women (Royal Free Hospital) for eleven years, and also served as a consulting surgeon at the Elizabeth Garrett Anderson Hospital. The Dictionary of National Biography notes that she was remarkable for her skills at boxing and cricket.

The bronze statue of Gandhi in the center of Tavistock Square is by the sculptor **Fredda Brilliant** (b. 1908), a multitalented woman who has been an actress and a scriptwriter as well as an artist. Her sculptural subjects have included Nehru, Paul Robeson, and Buckminster Fuller. If you should chance to be in Tavistock Square when Gandhi is surrounded by blazing red tulips, the scene is especially spectacular. Gandhi is depicted sitting cross-legged in a loin cloth, and the base of the statue contains a circular hollow for the offering of floral tributes.

On the northwest side of Tavistock Square lies Woburn House, where the entrance to the Jewish Museum† is located. The museum opened in 1932 and has over a thousand items relating to Anglo-Jewish history, some of which date back to the thirteenth century. It is filled with a fascinating clutter of portraits, scrolls, plate, hangings, and candlesticks. Among the museum's collection of portrait medallions is one depicting Sir Moses and Lady **Judith Montefiori*** (d. 1862). Lady Montefiori was a philanthropist in her own right, and also accompanied her husband on the travels he undertook on behalf of the Jewish cause in Europe, often at great personal risk. In 1836 she had privately printed *A Private Journal of a Visit to Egypt and Palestine by Way of Italy and the Mediterranean,* which she had written about their journeys. Another medal in the collection is of the Hon. **Lilian Montagu*** (1873–1963). In 1918 Montagu preached at London's Liberal Jewish Synagogue, thereby becoming the first woman of her faith to be formally received as a lay minister in England.

The museum's holdings include a collection of eighteenth-century handwritten and illuminated marriage contracts, which set out (in Hebrew) stipulations as to dowry and obligations, and a cabinet of miniatures contains a portrait of Abraham da Costa painted by his mother, **Catherine Da Costa** (1679–1756), who may have been the first Jewish woman artist in England.

From the northeast corner of Tavistock Square take Upper Woburn Place north to the broad and busy thoroughfare of *Euston Road* and turn right. On your right you will see St. Pancras Church, its Coade Stone caryatids now somewhat shabby. As you head east, the remarkable red neo-Gothic castle of St. Pancras Station will rise before you. Euston Road was built in 1756 by the second Duke of Grafton, who wanted to drive his cattle to the Smithfield Market without using Oxford Street and

Holborn. The Capper family tried to block the development, claiming in a petition to the House of Commons that the clouds of dust raised by the cattle would spoil their hay, but their efforts were in vain. The **Capper** sisters were known for their customary garb of riding habits and men's hats; they used to ride after boys flying kites and snip their strings with shears, or seize the clothing of those who trespassed to bathe on their land.

Where *Churchway* intersects Euston Road on the left you'll find the red and yellow brick buildings of the **Elizabeth Garrett Anderson*** Hospital, and if you walk a little way down Churchway, you can find a small plaque so identifying it. Anderson (1836–1917) began the hospital as a dispensary for women and children in 1866, after receiving her apothecary's certificate. Four years later she completed her ten-year struggle for a medical degree, receiving it from the University of Paris. Someone once asked her why she wanted to be a doctor instead of a nurse. "Because a nurse can earn £20 a year," she replied, "and a doctor £1,000." In recent years, the hospital has had to struggle to stay open.

Reverse your direction and head west on Euston Road, turning left into Gordon Street after passing Euston Station. This will take you into *Gordon Square*, a small, shady wilderness which is one of the nicest squares in London. The yellow stone of the University Church of Christ the King can be glimpsed through the leafy branches on the park's west side. On its east side, at No. 50, a plaque commemorates the "Bloomsbury Group," the intellectual and artistic circle of which **Virginia Woolf*** and her sister **Vanessa Bell*** were members. In fact, both sisters, along with their brothers Thoby and Adrian, lived at No. 46, where a plaque now commemorates the later residence of economist John Maynard Keynes (who was also a member of the Bloomsbury Group). Virginia and Vanessa lived there from 1905 to 1907, when they were still the Misses Stephens, and after her marriage to Clive Bell, Vanessa stayed on until 1916.

From the southwest corner of Gordon Square turn right into Byng Place, and glance across the street at *Torrington Square*, where the Victorian poet **Christina Rossetti** (1830–1894) once lived. Rossetti wrote sensuous, lyrical poems on both secular and religious themes, and also wrote works of devotional prose. Her health was poor and after 1876 she lived in a state of semi-seclusion.

In *Byng Place* itself, just past the phone kiosks, you will come to what is now Quaker International Centre. The Friends have had the building since the mid-sixties, but by that time it had been occupied by more than one group of enterprising women. In the 1880s the building was used as a "College Hall and Home for Ladies," run by the Misses **Brown,** and in 1913 it became a home for female students at the University of London, nearby University College, and the London School of Medicine for Women. In the 1930s it was purchased by Miss K. M. Courtauld on behalf of the Women's Farm and Garden Association, a group which had been founded in 1899 in order to foster agricultural careers among women. It was the Women's Farm and Garden Association which organized the Women's Land Army during the two world wars.

Diagonally across from Quaker International Centre (between Malet and Gower streets) is the Victorian Gothic edifice of Dillon's, where the poet Dame **Edith Sitwell*** (1877–1964) gave unscheduled recitations of her works to the bookstore's surprised customers. Sitwell was fond of making people sit up and take notice. During her Paris years she was part of Gertrude Stein's* unconventional circle, and she often wore remarkable costumes and jewelry. In her later life she made many television appearances. Her poems satirized societal corruption and dealt with the question of human suffering. She became a Roman Catholic in 1955.

Turn right (north) into *Gower Street*, and head north for a peek at the red Victorian Gothic buildings of University College. Here **Marie Stopes*** took degrees in geology, geography, and botany before going on to found a birth control clinic in 1921. A distinguished faculty member here was Dame **Kathleen Lonsdale** (1903–1971), who was, in addition to being a Professor of Chemistry, a Quaker and a pacifist. In 1943 she was sent to prison for refusing to register for war duties. University College is now part of the University of London.

Retrace your steps, heading south on gloomy Gower Street,

which is here dominated by bed-and-breakfast houses. A block before returning to Bedford Square you will pass the intersection of *Store Street*, which comes in from the west. The brick buildings and green and white shops give no indication of the fact that **Mary Wollstonecraft*** (1759–1797) lived here in 1792, when she wrote *Vindication of the Rights of Woman*. Wollstonecraft was not from an intellectual family. Largely self-educated, she began working as a companion in Bath before she was twenty years old. A few years later she and her intimate friend, Fanny Blood, founded a school in Newington Green. After Fanny's death she had an unhappy love affair with a man from the United States, Gilbert Imlay, to whom she bore a daughter (named Fanny). In 1795, unable to accept Imlay's constant infidelity, she tried to commit suicide by throwing herself off Putney Bridge. The following year she began living with William Godwin, and when she found herself pregnant, succumbed to public opinion by marrying him, against her principles. She died a few days after the birth of her daughter, later **Mary Shelley*** (1797–1881), the author of *Frankenstein*.

Throughout these years she wrote a number of books and essays, including *Thoughts on the Education of Daughters* and *History and Moral View of the Origins and Progress of the French Revolution*. But it was *Vindication of the Rights of Woman* which, in combination with her unconventional sexual mores, caused a scandal. In it she advocated equality of education for women, employment of single women, and companionship with, rather than subservience to, men. Many women consider it the founding literature of feminist theory.

At No. 10 *Gower Street* you will see a plaque noting the former residence there of Lady **Ottoline Morrell** (1873–1938). Morrell was a patron of the arts and a friend to Joseph Conrad, D. H. Lawrence, and Virginia Woolf*, among others. Woolf wrote of her, early in their acquaintance: "We have just got to know a wonderful Lady Ottoline Morrell, who has the head of a Medusa; but she is very simple and innocent in spite of it, and worships the arts."

At the foot of Gower Street, just before its intersection with Montague Place (opposite Bedford Square), you will find No. 2, where Dame **Millicent Fawcett*** lived and died. By the time the Pankhursts' WSPU came into being Fawcett had been working for the vote for over thirty years. Although in her memoirs she defended the militant movement against its critics, she also said gravely, "I could not support a revolutionary movement, especially as it was ruled autocratically." Fawcett was president of the National Union of Women's Suffrage Societies in 1908, when it broke with the WSPU over the issue of violence. She was the chief leader of what came to be called the "constitutional" wing of the women's suffrage movement.

Gower Street now becomes Bloomsbury Street, and if you follow it for a short distance it will deliver you to Great Russell Street, where you are once more at the British Museum.

2

Holborn

Begin and End: Holborn Tube Station

Holborn is a district most famous for its legal associations, and indeed, the Inns of Court—with their ancient brick, gas lamps, narrow passageways, and spacious greens—are among the marvels of London. It's easy to forget that, among other functions, the Inns served to exclude women from the legal profession in England until 1919. For women, the landmarks of Holborn have as much to do with literary and labor, as with legal, history.

From the tube station, walk south on *Kingsway*, that wide traffic artery that plunges toward the Strand. Almost immediately on the west side of the street you'll see the curved and stained facade of Holy Trinity Church, which stands on the site of a house in which **Mary Lamb*** (1764–1847) once lived. It was here that she stabbed her mother to death with a pair of scissors. The court found her insane and committed her to the care of her brother, the essayist Charles Lamb; thereafter they were inseparable. Lamb was good with children and enjoyed coauthoring *Tales from Shakespeare* with her brother; she also wrote a number of instructive tales for children. But she was subject to

21

fits of violence and was several times placed in a lunatic asylum. When she and Charles went on vacation, she is said to have packed her straightjacket among her clothes, just in case.

In 1922 **Dorothy Sayers*** (1893–1957) went to work at Benson's advertising agency in Kingsway. It was in this milieu that her lively mystery *Murder Must Advertise* is set, and the infamous spiral staircase on which the deceased met his fate was one she clattered up and down regularly in the course of her workday, her cloak streaming behind her.

Dorothy Leigh Sayers

Just east of Kingsway, and easily reached by a left turn onto Remnant Street (opposite Great Queen Street), lies *Lincoln's Inn Fields*, larger than a square, but not on a scale with London's great parks. The square was first laid out in 1613, and for a hundred years was notorious for the thieves, beggars, and sideshows which haunted its precincts. Today you may encounter members of London's homeless community taking their rest.

Powis House is the brick building in the northwest corner of the square, built in 1684–89 and since restored. The original Powis House, also in Lincoln's Inn Fields, was mentioned often in the trial of **Elizabeth Cellier*** for high treason in 1679. Cellier, a Catholic midwife, often consulted with **Elizabeth Powis** (d. 1693), whose husband the earl spent six years shut up in the Tower on conspiracy charges manufactured by Titus Oates ("the Popish Plot"). The subject of these consultations was disputed: Cellier claimed they had discovered a Puritan plot to assassinate the king; her chief accuser claimed Cellier herself was helping to plan the deed. Cellier defended herself cleverly, getting off, as it were, on a technicality, but she was certainly innocent of that particular charge. Later, when things had calmed down for Catholics under James II, Cellier proposed a "college for midwives" which would establish a means for women to improve their medical skills and help to keep the profession in the hands of women. But with the abdication of James in 1688, her hopes for the plan came to an end.

If you enter the park on its north side and proceed east, you'll come soon to a memorial to **Margaret McDonald** (1870–1911), one of the early leaders of the Labour Party, who lived with her husband Ramsay McDonald (first secretary of the Labour Party) at No. 3 Lincoln's Inn Fields. Her arms are stretched protectively over a group of children, emphasizing her lifelong concern for women's and children's issues. She fought for infant clinics and nursery schools, and worked to organize women through the National Federation of Women Workers. She was the first chairperson of the Women's Labour League, formed in 1906.

Directly opposite, on the south side of the park, stands the Royal College of Surgeons. It was on August 5, 1861, that a letter from **Elizabeth Garrett Anderson*** (1836–1917), then Elizabeth Garrett, was read at a meeting of the College's Council. The impertinent Miss Garrett wished her attendance of lectures to be registered, so that at the end of four years she would qualify to take the examination in midwifery. After due consideration the Council refused her request, but in 1876 the question arose again, when **Sophia Jex-Blake*** (1840–1912), **Edith Pechey** (1845–1908), and **Isabel Thorne** requested permission to enter for the examination in midwifery. After much discussion the Council gave its consent, only to find that the examiners resigned rather than act against their principles by administering the exam to women. Some questions were also raised about Jex-Blake's qualifications, and the Council made an about-face in the matter of women entrants. Jex-Blake eventually qualified via the Irish College of Physicians and became the first woman doctor in Scotland. It was through her influence that the Edinburgh Medical School at last opened its doors to women. As for the Royal College of Surgeons, it was not until 1909 that they admitted women to their elite society. By this time there were over 750 qualified medical women, and the approval of this august institution was only a frill. In 1926 restrictive clauses barring women from participation in the governing of the College were eliminated.

The College has been on this site since the early 1800s, but only the library and entrance hall date to the 1835 edifice; the rest has been rebuilt.

The Royal College of Surgeons is situated more or less where the Lincoln's Inn Fields Theatre once stood, between the southern perimeter of Lincoln's Inn Fields and Portugal Street. The theater was managed by actor Thomas Betterton and his wife, **Mary Saunderson Betterton** (1637?–1712). Betterton may have been the first woman to appear professionally on an English stage (not permitted until Charles II gave his royal leave in 1660), though the honor is claimed for both of the theater companies in existence at the time. Her marital status distinguished her from the majority of actresses in her day, who were kept women, and the fact that she was comanager of the theater enabled her to pay herself a staggering salary of fifty shillings a week in 1691. Betterton was also a teacher; she gave drama lessons to the princesses Anne* and Mary* at the court of Charles II, and also to Sarah Jennings, who was later Sarah Churchill*, Duchess of Marlborough. When her own acting career was over she turned to the training of younger actresses, including **Anne Bracegirdle*** (1663?–1748). Bracegirdle may have been another exception to the rule about the love life of actresses; history has argued heatedly about whether she was a discreet lover or a frigid flirt. While she was alive, there were rumors that she had secretly married the playwright William Congreve, who was besotted with her.

It was here that several of **Aphra Behn's*** plays were produced, including her first, *The Forc'd Marriage,* which opened in December of 1670, with a cast that included Mary Betterton. Behn was an enormously popular author. At a time when London had only two theaters, seventeen of her plays were produced in seventeen years, most of them here or at the Dorset Garden Theatre (which was off of Fleet Street, where the entrance to Salisbury Court is now). She wrote thirty novels, produced several collections of poems, and did translations. Her plays were severely criticized for being bawdy, "the least and most excusable fault in the men writers," as Behn wrote indignantly. She defended women's right to write and reminded women of their lost history:

> *We once were famed in story, and could write*
> *Equal to men; could govern, nay, could fight.*
> *We still have passive valour, and can show,*
> *Would custom give us leave, the active, too.*

Behn's own valor was not exclusively passive: She travelled to Antwerp as a spy for Charles II in the Dutch wars.

Another woman playwright who was criticized for bawdiness was **Mary Pix*** (1666–before 1709). Her play *The Innocent Mistress* was performed at Lincoln's Inn Fields in 1697, with a cast that included Elizabeth Barry* and Anne Bracegirdle. A contemporary critic said of the play, "Though the title calls this innocent, it deserves to be damned for its obscenity." In addition to comedies, Pix wrote a number of historical plays, some of them in verse.

Mary Delariviere Manley* (1663–1724) is one of the most fascinating of the "female wits" of the late seventeenth century. In addition to her plays—one of which was performed at Lincoln's Inn Fields in 1696—she wrote novels, satire and lampoons, and political propaganda for the Tories. She collaborated with Swift on pamphlets attacking Whig corruption and succeeded him as editor of the Tory political magazine, the *Examiner*, in 1711. (Swift said of her that she had "a great deal of good sense and invention; she is about forty, very homely and fat.") Manley's works repeatedly defend women who write and sympathize with "ruined" women (Manley herself was tricked into a bigamous marriage with a cousin in her youth), and one of her works includes one of the few literary accounts of lesbianism of her day.

In 1709, Manley was arrested for libel in connection with her work, *Secret Memoirs and Manners of Several Persons of Quality of Both Sexes from the New Atlantis,* and the publishers were prevented from distributing copies of its sequel. Lady Mary Wortley Montagu*, who was quite vexed not to receive the eagerly awaited continuation of satire and scandal, wrote to a friend: "Do you know what has happened to the unfortunate authoress? People are offended at the liberty she used and she is taken into custody! Miserable is the fate of writers! If they are agreeable they are offensive, and if dull they starve."

In *Portugal Street* itself, during the 1860s and 1870s, Miss **Maria Rye** (1829–1903), who was associated with the Society for Promoting the Employment of Women, ran an office where educated women could get work as copyists of legal documents.

To the east of Lincoln's Inn Fields lies Lincoln's Inn† itself, which was founded (at the latest) in the fourteenth century, at the time when the clergy ceased to practice law, and courtrooms were turned over to the new professionals. It was once customary for all barristers to study, live, and worship at the Inns of Court, sanctuaries from rough and tumble London. Now studies take place at universities, but the Inns are still in the hands of the legal profession, and it is still necessary for a law student to eat three dinners in a term at her or his Inn's Hall in order to qualify for the bar. The Inns of Court serve as the examining board for the legal profession and reserve the sole power of calling persons to the Bar in England and Wales.

Lincoln's Inn is supremely peaceful. Among its exquisite lawns and ancient Tudor buildings (it sustained the least damage of all the Inns of Court during World War II) you may rest a bit from the London rush, reflecting on how much women have struggled to earn some of that peace for themselves. It was in 1904 that **Christabel Pankhurst*** (1880–1958) was denied admittance to Lincoln's Inn on the basis of her sex. The following year she won an international prize for law, and in 1906 she completed her law degree, but she was never able to practice—formally. When arrested for the militant acts she performed as a suffragette, however, her eloquent self-defense and clever arguments showed her legal training.

Returning to Lincon's Inn Fields, turn right and follow Great Turnstile Street north to *High Holborn*, where the roar of traffic and dense pedestrian traffic provide a sharp contrast to the quiet Inn. It was here that the confectioners Edwin and **Susan Sawle** kept their shop in the early seventeenth century. They provided sweetmeats for the children of King James I, but they may also have provided something more sinister—to Sir Thomas Overbury, who was imprisoned in the Tower. Overbury died from poisoning, administered through the machinations of several people, including Anne Turner* and the Countess of Essex, Frances Howard*.

Turn right on High Holborn and walk east until you reach Gray's Inn Road. A few steps beyond its junction you will see the vast Gothic Revival edifice of redbrick and terra-cotta that is the Prudential Assurance building. In 1871 the company became one of the early employers to take advantage of female labor, which could be had at a very low rate. The first women clerks were required to be daughters of professional men. They were provided with the special benefits lady workers needed: a separate entrance and staircase, their own refreshment room, the use of a piano, and terraces on the roof where they could take the air.

Retrace your steps and turn north (right) onto *Gray's Inn Road*. The entrance to Gray's Inn† itself will be on your left (opposite

Baldwin's Gardens). The Inn suffered a lot of damage from bombs during World War II, so almost all its buildings are restored. The Hall, located in South Square, has been rebuilt in the original sixteenth-century style. It was here that Shakespeare's *Comedy of Errors* was first performed in 1594. That same year a black courtesan named **Luce Morgan,** also known as Lucy Negro, played the part of the abbess in a masque at the Gray's Inn Revels. The prostitutes arrested at "Black Lucy's" and sent to Bridewell for flogging may have been part of her establishment. At least two Shakespearean scholars believe that Morgan may have been the "Dark Lady" of Shakespeare's sonnets.

It was several centuries later, in 1903, that **Bertha Cave** sought admission as a student at Gray's Inn. When she was denied on account of her sex, she appealed the decision. The judges granted her five minutes to present her case, then decided against her without taking time to deliberate. **Rose Heilbron** (b. 1914) had better luck; she was awarded a scholarship to Gray's Inn and was called to the bar in 1939. In 1956 she became the first woman Recorder in the United Kingdom, and in 1975 she became Chairman of the Home Secretary's Advisory Group on Rape.

Returning to Gray's Inn Road, continue north, crossing Theobald's Road, until you come to its junction with Elm Street. Here, in a QAred brick building called Clovelly Mansions, short story writer **Katherine Mansfield*** (1888–1923) and her devoted friend **Ida Constance Baker*** (1888–1978), known to literary history as L. M., lived in 1911. Mansfield was born Kathleen Beauchamp in Wellington, New Zealand; she died of tuberculosis at Gurdjieff's Institute for the Harmonious Development of Man, at Fountainebleau, France, in 1923. During those thirty-four years of living she behaved as no daughter of a respectable New Zealand banker ever should. At age nineteen she was living on her own in London; at twenty she married George Bowden—but left before the wedding night was over. She lived with her second husband, John Middleton Murry, for six years (on and off) before tying the knot, and carried on a love relationship of twenty years' duration (on and off) with L. M. (When her mother found out about L. M., she sent twenty-year-old

Katherine to a curative spa; it was there that the stories that appeared in Mansfield's first book, *In a German Pension*, were written. Then Mrs. Beauchamp sailed home to New Zealand and cut her daughter out of her will.) Mansfield, however, did something more important than behave scandalously: She wrote exquisitely crafted short stories in which she attempted (in her own words) to "intensify the so-called small things, so that truly everything is significant." Virginia Woolf* wrote in her diary that Mansfield's was the only writing of which she had ever been jealous.

Mansfield and L. M. furnished their three-room flat with bamboo matting, scattered cushions, a roll-top desk, an armchair and a basket chair, a stone Buddha (before which Mansfield set a bowl of water with bronze lizards in it), a hookah, and a grand piano. It was in this flat that, according to L. M. , one of Mansfield's admirers threatened to shoot himself for love of her. Mansfield's reply: "Oh, but do have a piece of this melon first."

Return to Theobald's Road and turn right (west), and continue until you see *John Street* on your right (the grounds of Gray's Inn will be on your left). In the 1890s, John Street was the site of a home for employed and unemployed barmaids. **Emily Drake,** who testified about her hours and working conditions to the Select Committee on Shop Hours in 1892, lived here. The next street to your right as you continue along Theobald's Road will be *Great James Street,* a pretty street of houses from the 1720s. Some of the tall brick buildings have ornamental hoods over the windows. The mystery writer **Dorothy Sayers*** lived here in 1922; it was a convenient ten-minute walk from her job at Benson's in Kingsway.

From Theobald's Road turn left in *Bedford Row,* which is just opposite Great James Street. This broad street, lined with leafy trees, has houses from about 1700, now chiefly occupied by lawyers' offices. The women bookbinders union, which was part of the Women's Protective and Provident League, used to meet here. Bookbinding was a somewhat difficult trade for women to enter, but **Sarah Prideaux** (flourished 1890) helped open the field to members of her sex. Prideaux, who was both a book-

Charlotte Despard

binder and a printer, taught her trade to younger women and wrote works on bookbinding, including histories, which were used as standard texts for many years.

At the south end of Bedford Row turn right into Sandland Street, which after it crosses Red Lion Street becomes *Eagle Street*. This unprepossessing avenue was once home to a pub called the Griffin. Here two of the very earliest women's trade unions held their meetings in 1834: The Women's Grand Lodge of Operative Straw Plaiters, Servers, Bleachers, and Blockers; and the Operative Straw-Bonnet Makers. Both were affiliates of the Grand National Consolidated Trades Union, which, under Owenite influence, sought to recruit women on an equal basis with men.

Turn left into Red Lion Street to rejoin High Holborn, then go west (right), passing the tube station, until you reach Southampton Place (not Row). There turn right, then left through the archway into tiny *Barter Street*, where the Women's Freedom League once had its headquarters. The league was founded by **Edith How** (1880–1954), **Theresa Billington-Greig**,* and **Charlotte Despard*** (1844–1939) in 1907, as a democratic alternative to the Women's Social and Political Union, which was run by the autocratic Pankhursts. Despard opened one of the first child welfare centers in London; she was a theosophist, a vegetarian, and a member of the Independent Labour Party. With the Women's Freedom League she campaigned against women paying taxes, as they were unrepresented in Parliament. Later she became active in Sinn Fein, the Irish revolutionary group, and helped to found the Irish Workers' College in Dublin for the political education of workers.

The same year that she helped to found the Women's Freedom League, Theresa Billington (1877–1964) married F. L. Greig, and both parties thereafter used the hyphenated name Billington-Greig. Theresa later became very critical of the militant tactics of the suffragettes; she advocated nonviolent strategies and criticized the single-issue orientation of the women's movement. She wrote extensively on a wide variety of women's issues, including personal relations with men and the potential economic power women had in their role as consumers.

Retrace your steps to the junction of High Holborn and Kingsway, where you will find yourself once more at the Holborn tube station.

3
The City

The City is a dense amalgamation of history and high-rises. It is the original London, the very oldest part, and proves it through city livery companies, fragments of Roman wall, the Tower of London, and thoroughfares with medieval names such as Milk Street, Ropemaker Street, Amen Corner, Drapers Gardens. Sometimes the quaint names are attached to disappointing blocks of gray concrete and glass, but it must be remembered that the Great Fire of 1666 was not the only disaster to transform the face of London. More recently, bombing damage that occurred during World War II devastated historic churches, halls, and entire streets. The tourist must reconcile herself to finding old corners among the maze of modern buildings and learn to experience the charm of such surprises. In spite of everything, it is still the most fascinating part of London, and though it occupies only one square mile, I have had to divide the area into three walks in order to do justice to the history that mile evokes.

Walk One

Begin: St. Paul's Tube Station
End: Blackfriars Tube Station

"The building of St. Paul's is very fine but I don't like all the pigeons that are constantly flying about," wrote the New Zealand short story writer **Katherine Mansfield*** (1888–1923) on her first trip to London, in 1903. She was then not yet a short story writer, but only a fifteen-year-old schoolgirl writing home. "The service was fearfully impressive," she wrote of her visit. "The church was dim, and there was a wonderful anthem. It seems to go right through you, and made you quite choky."

To today's pilgrim, St. Paul's Cathedral† will probably seem at first more like a circus than a church; milling tourists, flashing cameras, and postcard stalls make this spot the hub of commotion and activity. But there's still room for reverence. The building itself, with its great dome resting upon a double layer of paired columns, has been called more than "very fine" by people who ought to know. The designer, Sir Christopher Wren, was not a woman, and there is absolutely no getting around the fact at this late date. But the crypt contains some monuments to fascinating females, and there is nothing to stop able-bodied persons of any gender from climbing to the Whispering Gallery to experiment with the amusing acoustics there.

The crypt, the most fruitful part of the cathedral for feminists, is a vast whitewashed labyrinth of massive piers and archways, said to be the largest crypt in Europe. Through occasional grates in the low ceilings you can see the feet of the tourists who are strolling over your head in the main part of the cathedral. It's convenient to use as landmarks the adjacent rooms housing monuments to Lord Nelson and the Duke of Wellington, which are central and conspicuous. Located in the little passageway between the two is the largest memorial to a woman to be found in St. Paul's: a marble-framed relief of **Florence Nightingale*** (1820–1910). She is depicted caring for a wounded soldier, and the caption reads "Blessed are the merciful," reminding us that her life has often been used as an example of charity and self-sacrifice. Self-sacrificing she may have been; she was also a highly able administrator. She brought the principles of hygiene and analysis of medical statistics to the field of public health nursing, and when the Nightingale School of Nursing was endowed with public funds, she used it to establish professional standards for the nursing profession. She was widely consulted on administrative matters by leaders in the health care professions and was architect of the Indian Sanitary Commission.

Around the corner from the Nightingale memorial, to the south (up three steps), a glass case is affixed to the wall with a book open within it and a plaque above it. This is a memorial to the women and men of the Air Transport Authority who died during World War II. The women's division of the ATA was founded by **Pauline Gower** (1910–1947), who had to do a lot of lobbying before permission was granted. Women were paid twenty percent less than male pilots doing equivalent work and had to pay for their own lodgings. The women began by ferrying single-engined Tiger Moth trainers to Scotland and the north of England, in journeys that took between a few days and two weeks, depending on the weather. Later they were permitted to fly larger planes, and by 1943 they were ferrying 120 different types of aircraft. In 1944 they began ferrying to liberated parts of the Continent.

One woman whose name is recorded in the book before you is **Amy Johnson** (1903–1941), the first woman in England to be granted an Air Ministry's ground-engineer's license (she also received a full navigation certificate). Before the war, she made a number of spectacular flights, including, in 1930, a solo flight to Australia in a tiny Moth with a Gipsy engine—a flight which took nineteen days. In 1931 she flew from Siberia to Tokyo in ten days, a record. In 1932 she broke the record, held by her husband, James Mollison, for a solo flight to Cape Town. (In 1938 the marriage was dissolved, and she resumed use of her maiden name.) Johnson joined the ATA is 1939, and was lost over the Thames estuary on January 5, 1941. She was one of fifteen women who died in the process of ferrying planes for the ATA.

Proceed east from the Duke of Wellington's tomb (that is, head in the opposite direction of Lord Nelson) into the chapel of

Amy Johnson

the Order of the British Empire (those in wheelchairs use side aisle on north), and you'll discover in the southwest quarter an interesting wall plaque to the memory of **Maria Hacket** (1784–1874). It was Hacket's aim in life to make sure that funds for church and cathedral choirs were not wrongly diverted, and the authorities at St. Paul's were among those she confronted in this campaign. The plaque assures us that before she died she saw "on all sides the success of her labours." You will be facing west as you read the plaque.

In the southeast corner of the chapel, in the same corner as her brother, Sir Christopher Wren, you will find the tomb of **Susannah Holder** (d. 1688), who "applied herself to the knowledge of medicinal remedies, wherein God gave her so great a blessing that thousands were happily healed by her and no one ever miscarried." Holder's memorial is relatively easy to find, because Wren's is marked on the floor plan you are given upon your entrance to the crypt.

If you return to Lord Nelson's tomb and then go north (up two shallow steps), you will find yourself in the treasury, where you'll find some exquisite embroidery on the copes, stoles, and mitres there displayed. Much of this work was probably done by women, and the most recent works actually credit the artists. You may see on exhibit the Hammersmith Cope, designed by **Susan Riley** in the early 1960s, and (up two more shallow steps) the fascinating Jubilee Cope (1975–1977), designed by **Beryl Dean**. The latter shows the spires of seventy-three London churches.

When you're leaving St. Paul's, be sure to look at the statue of **Queen Anne*** (1665–1714) which stands in front. The cathedral was finished during her reign, and it was at the opening ceremony that the queen and her intimate friend, **Sarah Churchill***, Duchess of Marlborough (1660–1744), had a final falling out. They had quarrelled before, and **Abigail Hill Masham*** was now the royal favorite. The duchess was so upset by being displaced that she wrote a letter to her sovereign accusing her of having an unseemly inclination toward her own sex, a charge to which Anne made no reply. On the occasion of the opening of St. Paul's, Sarah tried to force a reconciliation, but was so afraid of being overheard by others that at one point she hushed the queen sharply—a fatal error. You don't tell the reigning monarch to shut up and expect to remain a favorite.

The neighborhood around St. Paul's was once the center of the publishing trade in the City. It was in Johnson's Shop in *St. Paul's Churchyard* (on your right-hand side as you face Queen Anne's statue) that the feminist classic *Vindication of the Rights of Woman*, by **Mary Wollstonecraft*** (1759–1797), was published in 1792. After the Great Fire of 1666, many publishers moved one street north to Paternoster Row, and **Anne*** and **Charlotte Brontë*** stayed at the Chapter Coffee House there in 1848 when making a visit to their publisher.

To the left of St. Paul's as you face the cathedral you will see a flight of steps leading to *Paternoster Square*. (Those in wheelchairs can see the square by using the ramp in Ave Maria Lane, on the square's west side.) There you will find the bronze *Paternoster: Shepherd and Sheep*, by the sculptor **Elizabeth Frink*** (b. 1930). Frink also paints and has published etchings, but she is known chiefly for her sculptures, several of which can be found in London's streets. The male form, and especially the head, is her particular sculptural interest.

Leave by the ramp on the left (west) side of the square, which will take you to Ave Maria Lane. Beyond it you will see *Amen Corner* (private), where **Mary Ann Hughes** (1770–1853) once lived. Through her husband, a Canon Residentiary at St. Paul's, she became acquainted with Richard Barnham, also a canon, and to him she transmitted the ballads, ghost stories, and legends that later became the basis for his book, *Ingoldsby Legends*, published in the 1840s.

The entrance to the Stationers' Hall is on the west side of *Ave Maria Lane*, where it shares a corner with a parking lot. The building is not open to the public, but you can admire the stained glass windows as you meditate on the history of this City Livery Company. The Hall has been on this site since 1611, though the present building, rebuilt in 1673 after the Great Fire of 1666, has been refronted, added onto, and, after bombing damage in World War II, restored. It was just a month before the Great Fire that the guild admitted its first recorded female apprentice, **Joanna Nye.** Daughter of an Essex parson, she was apprenticed to Thomas Minshall, engraver. Two years later, **Elizabeth Latham,** bookseller, was admitted to the guild by patrimony, her father having been a member. Such admission included the right to take on apprentices and to hold a share in the company's English stock. The widow Mrs. Edward **Griffin** became a freewoman of the guild as early as 1627.

A concrete footpath leads south from the Hall to *Ludgate Hill*, where you will turn right (west). A Roman memorial to **Claudia Martina,** aged nineteen, was discovered on Ludgate Hill in 1806. The memorial was "erected by Aneccletus, slave of the province, to his most devoted wife," and is now in the Museum of London.

Just before reaching Ludgate Circus you'll pass under a bright blue railway bridge, and on the south (left) side of the stone wall of the passageway you'll see a dark, square plaque reading: "In a house near this site was published in 1702 the Daily Courant first London daily newspaper." The plaque does not mention that the paper was founded and edited by a woman, **Elizabeth Mallet.** However, shortly after its founding the paper passed into the hands of Samuel Buckley.

Before you turn left at Ludgate Circus, spare a glance to the right at *Farringdon Street,* which passes under the Holborn Viaduct. Here **Emily Faithful** (1835–1895) had a steam printing office in 1862. Faithful had become inspired upon learning of the role of women in the fifteenth-century printing industry, and in 1857 founded her own firm employing only women. In 1859 she became secretary of the first Society for Promoting the Employment of Women, and the following year she founded the Victoria Press which was housed at several London addresses over the course of the years. In 1862 she became Printer and Publisher in Ordinary to the Queen. Victoria Press did the printing for the *Englishwoman's Journal,* a women's movement periodical founded by **Barbara Bodichon*** (1827–1891) and others in 1858.

In 1886 **Annie Besant*** (1847–1933) chaired a meeting held in Farringdon Street about police harassment of open-air speakers. Besant was one of the most fascinating political and spiritual figures of her day. Her activities ranged from organizing the Match Girls' strike at an East End factory to the founding of Central Hindu College in Benares, India. She was a socialist, a theosophist, a follower of Krishnamurti, and an advocate of birth control and of Home Rule for India.

Ludgate Circus marks the spot where the Fleet Bridge once stood, connecting Ludgate Hill to Fleet Street by spanning the Fleet River. You'll see no trace of the river today. It was channeled underground in 1766, as it proved to be a serious health hazard due to uncontrolled dumping of refuge and sewage. However, the river still flows under Farringdon and New Bridge streets, and it's still used as a sewer.

Turn left into *New Bridge Street,* and you'll spot almost at once a passageway on the right-hand side of the street that leads, after a bit of winding around, to St. Bride's Church (stairs). The church was formerly called St. Brigit's, of which "Bride" is a variant, presumably after the Irish saint said to have founded a convent in Kildare. In fact, **Brigit*** was a Celtic trinity goddess: ruler, healer, and metalsmith, whose cult of priestesses was centered at the shrine in Kildare. There, it was said, cows never went dry, and shamrocks sprang up in the footprints of the goddess. With Brigit, the Church followed its common practice of creating saints from pagan goddesses. After bomb damage in 1940, excavations revealed the foundations of seven previous churches, the first of which was a sixth-century structure similar to a church of the same period built at Kildare, indicating that there is an ancient tradition connecting St. Bride's with the goddess/saint of Ireland. The crypt of the church now houses a museum.

In the churchyard of St. Bride's, in an unmarked grave, lies **Mary Frith** (1584–1659), called Moll Cutpurse. Frith, daughter of a shoemaker, didn't care for women's occupations, so she cut her hair, dressed in men's clothes, and frequented taverns and tobacco shops. She was required to do public penance for her ways in 1605, and wept bitterly, but according to some accounts it was only because she was "maudelin druncke." She claimed to have a knack for locating stolen property and criminals, but she probably practiced the arts of the underworld herself.

Back on New Bridge Street, continue south. Between Bridewell Place and Tudor Street, on the right-hand (west) side of the street, you'll find a plaque that notes the site of what was once Bridewell Palace. In 1553, the site was given over to the use of a hospital and a prison for petty offenders and "disorderly women" (often prostitutes). Prisoners were usually sent for short terms only, but the sentence invariably included flogging. Public floggings were held twice a week in front of the prison court and were administered on the bare back. In the early seventeenth century, a ducking stool and stocks were added to Bridewell's furnishings. Flogging of females was finally abolished in 1791.

Bridewell was named after a holy well dedicated to St. Bride, indicating another link between Christian traditions and the traditions of the goddess. Wells sacred to the goddesses Brigit,

Morgan, and Hel were such a widespread phenomenon that ecclesiastical authorities of the tenth century felt it was necessary to forbid "well-worshippings."

Among the women imprisoned at Bridewell in the seventeenth century was **Anna Trapnell,** a woman many believed to be a prophet. Trapnell experienced extended trances in which she sang hymns, preached, prayed, heard the voice of God, and saw visions. She was much consulted, but when in 1654 she had a vision of the death of Oliver Cromwell, the Lord Protector, she was committed to Bridewell. Huge crowds of her supporters swarmed around the prison, and the minister and elders of All Hallows, Barking, published a pamphlet in her defense. Two days after it appeared Trapnell was released.

In a short distance New Bridge Street intersects with Queen Victoria Street; here you will find Blackfriars tube station.

Walk Two

Begin: St. Paul's Tube Station
End: Bank Tube Station

From the St. Paul's tube station walk west on wide *Newgate Street,* which was once called Bladder Street because of its many butchers' stalls. You will soon pass on your right the ruins of Christ Church Greyfriars, originally built for the Franciscan friars of adjoining Greyfriars Monastery. (A blue plaque on the wall of the post office marks the site of the monastery.) From 1291, when the heart of **Eleanor of Provence** (1222–1291), wife of Henry III, was buried there, the church had the patronage of queens. **Marguerite of France** (d. 1318), Edward I's second queen, was responsible for the monastery's rebuilding, and in 1318 was buried before the high altar. Another benefactor was **Isabella of France** (1292–1358), variously called Isabella the Fair, the She-Wolf of France, and the Liberator. As her husband, Edward II, preferred men in his bed, she took Roger Mortimer as her lover. In 1326, with an army of three thousand men, she deposed her husband and had her son crowned king, and later arranged for the very brutal murder of Edward II. Edward III, instead of being grateful for his crown, had Mortimer hanged, confiscated his mother's wealth, and had her imprisoned in a castle in Norfolk, where he visited her two or three times a year out of filial duty. After thirty-one years of imprisonment she died and was buried here at Greyfriars Monastery, where Mortimer had also been buried.

Philippa of Hainault* (1314–1369), another benefactor of Greyfriars, got along rather better with her husband, that same Edward III. She ruled as regent in England when he was in France during the Hundred Years' War, even leading an army to Neville's Cross and there driving back the Scots. She also encouraged merchants from her native Flanders to settle in Norwich.

Where Newgate Street intersects *Old Bailey* you will find the Central Criminal Court, commonly called the Old Bailey after the street in which it lies. The bronze lady who brandishes a sword atop the green dome is, of course, Justice, and justice has been here meted out (and presumably denied) to women and men since the Old Bailey Sessions House was first established on an adjoining site in 1539. One of these women was the black woman **Elizabeth Smith,** who in 1787, with her common-law husband, Thomas, was tried for stealing a watch and a pair of stone knee buckles from one Mr. Jones. If found guilty, the couple would have been hung. But the jury mercifully convicted them of a lesser offense—the theft of thirty-nine shillings, not a capital crime.

The spectacular trial of the militant suffragette leader **Emmeline Pankhurst*** (1858–1928) also took place in the Old Bailey. Pankhurst was tried as an accessory before the fact to the act of damaging with explosives the unoccupied country home of Lloyd George, who was chancellor of the exchequer at that time. On April 2, 1913, the day of the trial, the courtroom was packed with women, and many more waited out on the street to hear the outcome. Pankhurst gave a stirring speech in her own defense, saying, "I ask you if you are prepared to send an incalculable number of women to prison . . . because that is what is going to happen." Pankhurst was sentenced to three years penal servitude. Upon hearing this verdict, the women in the courtroom cried out in anger and at length filed from the court singing the

"Women's Marseillaise." When Pankhurst left the court at three o'clock that day by a side entrance in Newgate Street, accompanied by two women wardens, she found a crowd of women cheering her on. Many of them followed her in taxicabs to Holloway Prison, where she promptly began a hunger strike.

It used to be that prison was handier: From the twelfth century until 1902, the site where the court now sits was occupied by a prison. Newgate Prison, rebuilt in 1672 after the Great Fire, was a magnificent building lavishly adorned with sculpture and statues, but it had an inadequate water supply and almost no ventilation. The keeper and turnkeys made large profits from the selling of food, water, candles, and liquor to the prisoners. **Elizabeth Cellier*** was a Catholic midwife who visited and ministered to those of her own faith who were imprisoned during the hysteria surrounding the Popish Plot in 1678. She was appalled by the deplorable conditions that existed in Newgate. On one visit, she heard terrible screaming, and assuming that what she heard was a woman in labor, she offered her services which were declined. It was on this ground that she claimed that torture, which had been outlawed some years before, was still being carried out at Newgate. The pamphlet in which she described the horrors of the prison caused her to be sued for libel, and she was fined £1,000 and sentenced to stand three separate days in the pillory.

When the Quaker **Elizabeth Fry*** (1780–1845) came to visit the female prisoners in Newgate in 1813, more than a hundred years later, things had not improved much, in spite of the fact that a new prison had been built in 1778. But Fry's efforts to improve conditions were somewhat more effectual than Cellier's had been. She established a school in the prison for the children of imprisoned women, and persuaded the authorities to use enclosed hackney coaches to transport women convicts from the prison to the ships that were headed for Botany Bay. Previously the women had ridden chained and cuffed in open carts, vulnerable to the scorn of the public.

Newgate at one time included a gallows. **Catherine Hayes,** who murdered her husband, burned here in 1726. It was customary to be strangled by the hangman before the flames grew

Elizabeth Fry

too fierce, but in this instance the executioner's hand was burnt and he dropped the rope. The coin clipper **Christian Murphy** was also hanged at Newgate.

From Newgate Street turn right on *Giltspur Street,* which continues Old Bailey to the north. This will take you past St. Bartholomew's Hospital where Dr. **Elizabeth Blackwell** (1821–1910), the first woman on the British medical register, once studied. Blackwell received her initial medical training in New York but later lived in London, and in 1875 was appointed professor of gynecology at the London School of Medicine for Women.

Continue on Giltspur Street until it ends at Little Britain, just at the gates of the church of St. Bartholomew the Great. Barring the chapel in the White Tower, this dark and weathered church is the oldest place of worship in London, and parts of it date back to the twelfth-century Augustinian priory founded on the site. It was outside St. Bartholomew the Great that **Anne Askew***(1521–1546) was burned at the stake in 1546. She had to be taken to the stake in a chair, since her body had been so crippled from its torture on the rack. Another martyr from the same era was **Joan Boucher** (d. 1550), or Butcher, who was arrested for being an Anabaptist and for claiming that Christ "had not taken the flesh of the Virgin." She refused to recant, and was burned on May 2, 1550. She went to her death screaming and cursing.

Leave the churchyard on its north side and turn right into Cloth Fair, which will preserve you from modernity for a little while longer. Eventually, however, you'll have to jog left into Cloth Street, right into Long Lane, and finally, at the gates of the Barbican, right (south) into *Aldersgate*. From there, follow the signs toward the Museum of London to its entrance in Shaftesbury Place.

The Museum of London† presents a fascinating chronicle of the everyday life of Londoners, beginning in pre-Roman times and moving through to the present. Among the Roman remains are some stone images taken from Celtic shrines that depict the triple goddess worshipped in Celtic Britain (of which Brigit* was one manifestation). Also on display are leather bikinis worn by women athletes and entertainers during the Roman era. For the next thousand years or so, the items relating specifically to women are rather sparse. (The rooms devoted to Stuart times include an exhibit on witchcraft, though it's disappointingly small.) But the rooms dealing with the nineteenth and twentieth centuries chronicle many of the important changes in the everyday lives of women. *The House and Its Servants* tells a little of what it was like to be a woman in domestic service, and the Imperial Capital area includes an exhibit on women's growing participation in open-air exercise, from croquet to cycling. There are several displays relating to working women, including pictures of women in the East End and a cabinet containing an early typewriter and switchboard. Feminist travellers will take special pleasure in seeing the suffrage memorabilia on display, which includes photographs, posters, buttons, and postcards.

Leaving the museum, you will want to walk east on London Wall, which sounds romantic but is for the most part a shockingly modern maze of overpasses and high-rises. However, on your left you will in fact see a section of the Roman Wall. Continue on until you reach Wood Street. There turn left, then left again into *Monkwell Square*. The brick building of the Barber Surgeons' Hall, which replaces one destroyed in World War II, was opened in 1969. But the Barber-Surgeons Company has been in Monkwell Square since the mid-fifteenth century. Even earlier— as early as 1390—the guild had "Free Sisters," and its earliest charter had a special clause relating to the membership of women. Originally barbers assisted monks in surgery, then took over when monks were forbidden surgical practice.

Return to London Wall, crossing the street to its south side and continuing east until you see the City Business Library. Turn right just before it, walking through to Aldermanbury Square and then heading toward the green fountain to your left. In the courtyard above the fountain (stairs) you will find a thought-provoking sculpture of two large nudes, one of each sex, called *Beyond Tomorrow*. The group was created by **Karin Jonzen*** (b. 1914), who was born in London of Swedish parents and studied at the Slade School of Art before continuing her training in Stockholm.

Back by the fountain, continue south into *Aldermanbury Street*. It was here that the Anti-Slavery Society had its headquarters in 1828, when **Mary Prince,** a black woman from Antigua, came to them seeking help. She had been brought to London by her owners, Mr. and Mrs. Wood, but had been thrown out into the street for refusing to do any more laundry work—chilling and backbreaking labor which, in her already poor state of health, was nearly killing her. What Mary Prince wanted was a way to return to the West Indies so that she could rejoin her husband, who was a free man there. The Anti-Slavery Society tried to persuade Wood to sell her to those who would grant her her freedom, but he spitefully refused. In 1831, a pamphlet entitled

The History of Mary Prince, a West Indian Slave, Related by Herself, was published in London. One wishes that the scribes of this as-told-to book hadn't gone to such pains to Anglicize Prince's language. But in any case the narrative is a valuable, though horrifying, document of slave life in the West Indies. Mary Prince eventually became a domestic servant in London; it is unlikely that she ever saw her husband again.

At the south end of the street, on the left-hand side, a series of arches leads you from the modern buildings of Aldermanbury Street into a courtyard of buildings from the past. One of these is the Guildhall†, parts of which date back to the fifteenth century. The participation of women in guilds was probably more common in the Middle Ages than later on. In 1880 a report by the Royal Commission declared that "from the mention of Sisters in nearly all the returns of the Livery Companies it may be inferred that women were equally eligible with men for membership." Not all guild members, whether men or women, were practitioners of the craft or trade their guild governed, but many certainly were, and there is evidence that there were practicing female members of the Goldsmiths', Stationers', and Barbers' companies, among others. In 1770 the Gunmakers' Company listed a woman apprentice in its rolls, and in the early 1800s **Catherine Christopher** became a Free Sister of that guild. The brewers company may have been at one time largely female, as the feminine form of the word, "brewster," is found frequently in the records. But by the seventeenth century things had changed: In 1639 one **Mary Arnold** was sent to jail for continuing to brew in spite of a guild prohibition, and by the end of the century women were excluded from that company.

The banqueting hall (three steps up) is a gigantic dining room with an ecclesiastical air to it. A plaque on the north wall (on your left-hand side as you enter, toward the front of the hall) mentions famous trials held at the Guildhall in earlier times, including those of Lady **Jane Grey*** (1537–1554) and **Anne Askew***. Askew distinguished herself by very clever handling of her interrogators at her trial, but was not able to save herself from being burnt at the stake at the age of twenty-five.

A more modern event at the Guildhall was the Lord Mayor's

banquet for cabinet ministers held on November 9, 1909. Disguised as charwomen, suffrage leader **Alice Paul** (1885–1977) from the United States and English suffragist **Amelia Brown** entered the building early in the morning with buckets and brushes, then hid themselves and waited. When evening came, they stood in the gallery outside the banqueting hall, waiting until Herbert Henry Asquith, the Prime Minister, stood to speak. Brown then used her shoe to smash through the stained glass window separating the women from the banquet hall, and both suffragists shouted "Votes for women!" at the gathering below. One hopes the cabinet ministers all got indigestion from having their dinner spoiled, but they can't have fared as badly as did Brown. She was sent to prison for her act, where she followed the standard suffragette policy of going on a hunger strike. She was forcibly fed and as a consequence developed gastritis.

The Lord Mayor's banquet, held annually in the Guildhall, dates back to at least 1501. In 1983 the ancient tradition had a new twist: Both Prime Minister **Margaret Thatcher*** (b. 1925) and her host, Lord Mayor **Mary Donaldson*** (b. 1921), were women.

Back in Aldermanbury Street, turn right (west) onto Gresham Street, follow it to *Foster Lane*, and turn left. Foster Lane once glittered with goldsmiths' and jewellers' shops, and the Goldsmiths' Hall is still here, on the left-hand side of the street. The present building dates from 1835, but the company's history is much longer and is studded with female participation. Its records list 142 women who began apprenticeships with the guild, though only nineteen became "freemen by servitude" through completing those apprenticeships. (Some may have gone into the trade without benefit of full guild membership.) The rolls list 160 women silversmiths who registered their own marks, which were then stamped on any pieces wrought in their shops. The first woman to register her mark, **Agnes Harding,** did so in 1513. Some of the pieces done by **Ann Tanqueray,** a widow who registered her mark in 1720, are presently in the Hermitage Museum in Leningrad. **Hester Bateman** (1709–1794), whose sons preferred to work as journeymen to her rather than setting up shop on their own, entered her mark in 1761, and spent the next twenty-nine years turning out simple, neoclassical works that are great favorites with collectors today. She also made sacred plate for Jewish and Christian use.

Upon reaching *Cheapside,* turn left and walk east, staying on the left-hand side of the street. If you're here on a weekday, the street will be crowded with jostling shoppers and members of the City's work force, though Cheapside is no longer London's principle market as it was in medieval days. Colorfully named streets nearby mark the areas where various workers carried on their trades: the bakers in Bread Street, the dairy workers in Milk Street, the fishmongers in Friday Street, and so forth. In those times, water conduits stood at each end of the street, and when Edward I first brought his beloved queen **Eleanor of Castile*** to London, they flowed with wine instead of water. The "Cheapside Cross" which once stood at the corner of Cheapside and Wood Streets was one of the Eleanor crosses which marked the places where the queen's body lay in rest during its long funeral procession from Lincolnshire to Westminster Abbey. The cross, three stories high, was destroyed by the Puritans during the English Civil War.

In medieval times the paving stones of Cheapside were sometimes scattered with sand for jousting tournaments (so that the horses wouldn't slip). On one occasion, when **Philippa of Hainault*** and her ladies-in-waiting were in attendance, the stand from which they watched collapsed. Only Philippa's intervention saved the carpenters from severe punishment. A stone stand was built to replace the wooden one, and when the church of St. Mary-le-Bow (on your right-hand side) was designed by Wren after the fire of 1666, a balcony was added as a symbolic reminder of the old stone grandstand.

After Cheapside becomes Poultry (the street where poulterers once plied their trade, naturally) you will come to the entrance of *Old Jewry Street,* named for its medieval inhabitants. (The street will be on your left-hand side.) A synagogue once stood in the northwest corner of the street. The pressure on Jews to convert to Christianity was very strong in the Middle Ages, and Jews who refused to give in to it sometimes resented those who did. One such convert, **Juliana,** lived in Coleman Street, the northern extension of Old Jewry. She was entrusted by some monks with a child named Rose for the purpose of instructing her in the Christian faith. According to Juliana's story, some Jews kidnapped Rose and took Juliana herself to the home of the widow **Antera** in Old Jewry, where Antera placed a rope around Juliana's neck and threatened her with death if she didn't return to Judaism. She stopped short of carrying out her threat, however, and Juliana was put on a ship to be sent to France. She then made a dramatic escape, returned to London, and pressed charges against Antera and others. The defendants denied the story absolutely, and Juliana eventually withdrew her accusations. One wonders what really occurred.

In 1262, the street was ransacked, and over five hundred Jews were murdered because a Jew was said to have charged a Christian more than the legal interest allowed on a debt. Twenty-nine years later all Jews were expelled from England.

Continuing on Poultry, you will soon pass a small and unprepossessing street called *Grocers' Hall Court*. It was just east of here that Poultry Compter, a sheriff's prison, once stood. In the slave era, apprehended runaways were often sent to Poultry Compter to await shipment to the West Indies or the North American colonies. Shortly before 1690, one **Katherine Auker** was imprisoned there. She had committed the grave crime of having become a Christian and had been baptized in St. Katharine's by the Tower (since replaced by St. Katharine's Docks). Although English law was somewhat vague, there was some support for the idea that only heathen blacks could be slaves and that baptism would automatically secure one's freedom. Incensed by her act, Auker's owners, Mr. and Mrs. Rich of Barbados, tortured her, turned her out, then had her arrested as a runaway. They then left for Barbados without giving Auker a discharge which would allow her to work for someone else. In 1690, Auker petitioned Middlesex Sessions, and the court told her she could legally go into service elsewhere—but only until Robert Rich returned to England.

The next street on your left as you continue on Poultry is *St. Mildred's Court*, and at its entrance you'll see a plaque marking the spot where **Elizabeth Fry*** (1780–1845) once lived. Fry dedicated most of her life to prison reform, but she was also a married woman. When Joseph Fry asked her to marry him, when she was twenty years old, she inquired of him whether a married woman could have any other vocation besides the duties of a home. "Yes, if she were *my* wife," he said, and she took him at his word. (The New England Quaker and feminist Lucretia Mott*, who had come to London to attend the World Anti-Slavery Convention of 1840, was impressed with Fry's work but not with her person. "Unassuming, meek—modest—nothing very striking," Mott wrote in her diary.)

You are now at the many-spoked intersection that is the heart of the City. The *Mansion House,* the grand building on the south side adorned with Corinthian columns, is the official residence of the Lord Mayor of London. London has been electing its Lord Mayor (through a council of Aldermen) since 1215, and until recently it has been a strictly male post. But on Michaelmas Day (September 29) of 1983, Lady **Mary Donaldson*** was elected the first woman Lord Mayor in the City's history. Previously she had been the first woman sheriff.

The building, begun in 1793, includes a Justice Room, beneath which are nine cells for men and one for women. The latter, known as "the bird cage" because of its resemblance to same, was once occupied by the suffragette leader **Emmeline Pankhurst***.

The vast edifice on the north side, fronting Threadneedle Street, is the *Bank of England*. This august institution was first penetrated by women in 1894, when the first lady clerks were hired. They were admitted by nomination only, and only twenty-five of them. Until World War II a female clerk at the Bank could not go from one part of the building to another without a chaperone. Adorning the pediment of the Bank's facade is "the Old Lady of Threadneedle Street," a nickname for the bank itself coined by Richard Brinsley Sheridan in 1797. She holds a model of the building on her knee.

Extending almost due east from Poultry is *Cornhill Street*, once the home of the publishers Smith and Elder, whose clients included the Brontës and the novelist **Elizabeth Gaskell*** (1810–1865). At No. 32, on the right-hand side of the street, you will find double doors bearing carved wooden panels which depict scenes from the city's history. The top panel on the right-hand door shows **Eleanor,** Duchess of Gloucester (d. 1447), performing a penance by walking barefoot through the city in 1441. Eleanor's crime was witchcraft, specifically, trying to bring about the death of Henry VI by burning a wax image of the king. After her penance she was banished from London.

The bottom panel of the same door shows the **Brontë*** sisters, **Charlotte** (1816–1855) and **Anne** (1820–1849), visiting their publishers in Cornhill Street. The visit was prompted by a rumor that in fact there was only one author involved in the writing of the books that had been published under the names Currer, Ellis, and Acton Bell. Anxious to establish their bona fides, Charlotte and Anne revealed their gender in order to prove that two of them, at any rate, existed.

Retreat to the heart of the intersection and turn sharply left into Lombard Street to find the impressive church of *St. Mary Woolnoth* (stairs). The elaborate interior includes a blue ceiling starred with gold, crystal chandeliers, and a plaque to John Newton, whose sermons in the late eighteenth century inspired the playwright **Hannah More*** (1745–1833) to give up the theater and pursue a life of good works. In *King William Street* itself, in about 1900, could be found the Enterprise Club, a City Club for Lady Clerks. The club had approximately two hundred members and provided a library, common rooms, inexpensive meals, an employment registry, membership in the Chess Circle and Ladies Hockey Club, the opportunity to learn French or woodcarving, and a chance to go on inexpensive group holidays.

If you're ready to call it a day, the Bank Street tube station is another useful feature of that many-spoked intersection. If not, the starting point for the third City walk is only a few blocks away.

Walk Three

Begin: Monument Tube Station
End: Tower Hill Tube Station

Five years after the Great Fire of 1666, the civic authorities decided that something substantial was needed to mark its calamitous point of origin, and Sir Christopher Wren was commissioned to design what is now called simply "the Monument." You'll find it by looking up—it's the tall column topped with a golden flame, which stands at the end of *Fish Hill Street*. The 202-foot column of Portland stone is just 202 feet from Pudding Lane, where the fire is believed to have begun. The translation of the Latin inscription indicates that the Monument† was intended to appease God, to prevent any further catastrophes.

If you climb the 311 narrow steps to the viewing platform you will be following in the footsteps of **Annie Barnes,** who was a new member of Sylvia Pankhurst's* East London Federation in or about the year 1913. Her first assignment was to scatter suffrage leaflets from the top of the Monument, and she performed it boldly. When she came down, a police officer was waiting to arrest her, but she assured him that the deed was perpetrated by another young woman who was still up there, and hurried away, leaving him to await the phantom suffragette. (The viewing platform was encaged in 1842, after a woman who was a domestic servant became the sixth person to commit suicide by throwing herself from the Monument.)

Use Fish Hill Street or Pudding Lane to join Eastcheap, and follow it east as it becomes Great Tower Street and then Byward Street. Here turn left (north) into *Seething Lane*. The street is now completely respectable, but in the early seventeenth century prostitutes were taken from Diogenes' House in Seething Lane to Bridewell, where they were flogged. Midway down the street is a small park ornamented by a larger-than-life-sized bronze of Samuel Pepys, the seventeenth-century diarist. The work was created by the sculptor **Karin Jonzen*** (b. 1914). At the north end of the street you'll find the church of St. Olave's (three steps down), where Pepys was a regular worshipper. His diary is rife with accounts of his womanizing but also with anecdotes of his wife, **Elisabeth Pepys** (1640–1669), who was not exactly meek. On one occasion she came at him with red-hot pincers in revenge for his having pulled her nose the day before. Another time he complained that she had called him a "pricklouse" (a derogatory reference to his humble origins in a tailor's family), and once he mourned that, after she had been to the public baths, she forbade him her bed until he made some similar improvement to his own person. He was very cold at night until he broke down and bathed himself in warm water, after which Elisabeth relented.

As you stand facing the altar, you can see a bust of the animated Elisabeth on the left-hand side of the nave, high on the wall.

Also worth noting in St. Olave's is the large stained glass window at the front of the east aisle (to the left of the altar when facing it). Seven women of renown are shown on the window. The three large figures in the foreground are **Elizabeth I*** (1533–1603), St. **Mary**, and St. **Catherine;** above these are shown **Elizabeth Fry,* Florence Nightingale*** (1820–1910), **Edith Cavell*** (1865–1915), and **Josephine Butler** (1828–1906). Butler spent many years working for the repeal of the Contagious Diseases Act of 1864, which provided for the compulsory medical examination of women suspected of being prostitutes. The law was applied chiefly to garrison towns and seaports, resulting in humiliation and punishment for the women involved, but no penalties of any kind for the men. It was at last repealed in 1886. Butler also founded a home for "fallen women" and helped to expose child prostitution; through her influence the laws regulating vice were reformed in Switzerland, Holland, Norway, France, and Italy. She wrote a number of books, including a biography of Catherine of Siena which was published in 1898.

Retrace your steps down Seething Lane and make your way along Tower Hill Street to the *Tower of London*.

The Tower: Castles of gray stone rise beyond a grassy moat; the Tower Green sparkles; ravens flap suddenly and caw raucously. Beyond the Tower's precincts the Thames flows under the fairylike Tower Bridge. The scene is ancient, awesome, and evocative. It has been palace, prison, and zoo, and now it is—practically speaking—a museum, and above all sights in London, the one not to be missed.

It is in its incarnation as a prison that the Tower is richest in history (alas, all the names of the female lions and tigers have been lost, another blow to women's studies). The most famous women associated with the Tower, of course, are the queens, two of whom lost their royal heads on Tower Green, where private executions of the very privileged took place. These were **Anne Boleyn*** (1507–1536) and **Catherine Howard** (1522–1542), Henry VIII's unsatisfactory wives. **Jane,** Viscountess Rochford (d. 1542), who died upon the same day as Howard, was the queen's lady-in-waiting.

The seventeen-year-old Lady **Jane Grey*** (1537–1554) also died on Tower Green. She had been proclaimed queen by the machinations of her husband, Lord Guildford Dudley, and her father-in-law, but her "reign" only lasted nine days. It is doubtful that Grey had much interest in being queen, but she was much admired by the scholars of her day for her proficiency in Latin, Greek, Hebrew, Italian, and French.

Margaret Pole, Countess of Salisbury (1473–1541), was sixty-eight when she was executed on Tower Green. The beefeater guide may tell you that she was executed because Henry VIII couldn't get hold of her son. It is certainly true that it was Reginald's religious book *De Unitate Ecclesiastica*, which he injudiciously sent to Henry from the safety of Italy, that aroused the king's killing wrath. But it was not the first time she had proven an annoyance to the head of the royal family. As Princess Mary's governess, she had been dismissed for refusing to give Mary's jewels into the keeping of the representative of the new queen (Anne Boleyn), and following her dismissal she declared that she would follow and serve the princess at her own expense. When she was arrested, she refused to admit any treasonous acts, but papal bulls and certain incriminating letters were found among her things, and it is safe to say that she was not happy about Henry's ecclesiastical independence from Rome.

One royal visitor to the Tower who left with her neck intact was the Princess **Elizabeth***, who was suspected by her half-sister Mary of being involved in a Protestant plot to gain the throne. Elizabeth entered by Traitor's Gate, then accessible by boat—as did Boleyn, Howard, and Lady Jane Grey. She was quartered in the Bell Tower, and is said to have taken exercise by walking on the ramparts between Bell and Beauchamp towers. When Elizabeth was herself queen, she took her turn at imprisoning others, including the Lady **Katherine Grey** (1540–1568), Jane's sister, who had married without Elizabeth's consent. Katherine was pregnant when sent to the Tower, and gave birth there, living fairly comfortably in the meantime with her collection of parrots, monkeys, and lapdogs. Sir Edward Warner, governor of the Tower, occasionally let the forbidden husband visit his wife, and lost his job when Katherine became pregnant a second time. Lady Katherine ought to have taken the advice of **Blanche Parry,** chief gentlewoman of the Privy Chamber under Queen Elizabeth. She was a noted palmist and crystal gazer, and had warned Lady Katherine not to marry without the queen's consent.

A more treacherous form of witchcraft was the alleged crime of **Jane Shore** (d. 1527), wife of a goldsmith in Lombard Street. Shore had been mistress to Edward IV (having petitioned for an annulment of her marriage on the ground that her husband was impotent). According to Sir Thomas More, Shore had "a proper wit" and could read and write. After Edward's death, the Duke of Gloucester, later Richard III, accused "Shore's wife" and others of sorcery. Her goods were confiscated, and she was imprisoned in the Tower. However, Richard's own prosecutor became quite charmed with Jane Shore, and in the end all Richard could manage was to have her brought as a harlot before the Bishop of London. She was forced to do public penance, walking barefoot through the filthy London streets dressed in a smock and carrying a candle.

Less famous women prisoners in the Tower include **Pimenta,** wife of Jacob of Coutances, and her daughter-in-law **Belicate.** These medieval Jewish women of Bristol had been charged with murdering a Christian woman. They escaped capture and fled to London, but they were arrested there and imprisoned in the Tower. Another little known prisoner was **Catherine Bellamy,** who was sent to the Tower under sentence of death for harboring Jesuits. She died there in 1586.

In addition to those women who entered the Tower as prisoners, there were those who came to visit. Sir Thomas More's daughter, **Margaret Roper*** (1505–1544), often visited her father in the Bell Tower. There is a story that when he was executed, she retrieved his head from its pike on London Bridge—an act very strictly forbidden. The heads were generally left to rot, sometimes staying up nearly a century. Lady **Winifred Maxwell,** who visited her husband Lord Nithsdale at the Queen's House in 1716, must have been a very welcome visitor indeed. She came accompanied by her ladies-in-waiting, all of whom were wearing extra clothing, and Lord Nithsdale, who had been condemned to death for his part in a Jacobite uprising, was able to dress himself in female clothing and escape. He eventually reached Rome and his wife joined him there; she later penned a narrative describing the daring escape.

The Crown Jewels, displayed now in the Upper and Lower chambers of the Jewel House, date primarily to the seventeenth century. Relics of queens include the crown, sceptre, and ivory rod of **Mary of Modena** (1658–1718), consort of James II, and the orb and sceptre of **Mary II*** (1662–1694), who reigned jointly with her cousin and husband William III after deposing her father, James II, in 1688. Mary II had an intimate friend named **Frances Apsley** to whom she was much attached; she once wrote this amusing and touching note to her: "I am more in love with you every time I see you, and love you so well that I cannot express it no way but by saying I am your louse in bosom and would be very glad to be always so near you."

In January of 1913, as part of an unprecedented suffragette campaign that included arson, the destruction of paintings in museums, and the sending of red pepper mixed with snuff to cabinet ministers, a Mrs. **Cohen** of Leeds smashed one of the jewel cases in the Tower of London. Security precautions today pretty much rule out that particular form of militancy.

A few blocks from the Tower you'll find the Tower Hill tube station, on the District and Circle lines.

4

The East End

The East End—an area that encompasses Whitechapel, Spital-fields, Shoreditch, Bethnal Green, Hackney, Stepney, Shadwell, Limehouse, and Poplar—is every bit as filled with history as the better-known districts in central London. But the associations are different ones. Where Mayfair means rich, the East End means poor; where Covent Garden means theatrical history, the East End means labor history.

As the traditional home of the poor and working classes of London, the East End has also been home to wave upon wave of immigrants, including French Huguenots, the Irish, Jews, Chinese, West Indians, and Pakistani. European Jews constituted by far the largest immigrant group. The first immigrants were Sephardic Jews fleeing the Inquisition in Spain and Portugal; later Ashkenazi Jews sought refuge from persecutions in France, Germany, and Poland. But it was not until the last quarter of the nineteenth century that bloody pogroms in Russia and Poland brought Jews to London's East End in truly staggering numbers.

The women who arrived at the docks were often poor and spoke no English; they were a vulnerable target to procurers who offered cheap lodgings or claimed to be delivering messages from relatives, in order to kidnap the women into a slavery of prostitution. The Hebrew Ladies' Protective Society regularly sent representatives to the docks to warn new arrivals against this danger. In 1909, a conference of the Jewish Association for the Protection of Girls and Women reported that there had been 222 cases of women "who have taken to immoral lives" during the years 1903–1909. Many of these women had disappeared completely from the country.

By the time of the great Jewish influx the French Huguenots had been completely assimilated into Britain, but the Jews competed for jobs with a more recent immigrant group—the Irish, who had come in large numbers at the time of the potato famine in 1848. Irish girls often sold flowers or vegetables, or, if an unwed loss of virginity resulted (as it usually did) in social ostracism, they turned to prostitution. Streetwalkers wore red bandanas about their necks and carried canes for easy identification. Ratcliffe Highway, near Limehouse, was their particular haunt, and a newspaper article of 1857 complained of women "who, wildly drunk, are walking [six] abreast occupying the whole of the footway, and singing, or rather screeching, snatches of obscene songs at the very tops of their voices."

The most recent wave of immigrants came from Bangladesh (East Pakistan). The men came first, arriving in the fifties as guest workers to help solve the labor shortage. Later, as the shortage disappeared and authorities began to discuss immigration quotas, they sent for their wives and families. Gradually a Pakistani colony grew up in the East End, which has faced the same difficulties of poverty and persecution that every immigrant group—except the popular Huguenots—has faced.

The East End has been the site of much exciting feminist and labor activity on the part of working-class women, some of which centered around the East London Federation of the Suffragettes, founded by **Sylvia Pankhurst*** (1882–1960). Originally a chapter of the Women's Social and Political Union, from the beginning the Federation didn't quite fit in with the rest of the WSPU. For one thing, the chapter made its decisions democratically, whereas Christabel* and Emmeline Pankhurst* liked

Sylvia Pankhurst

women who took their orders from the top. For another thing, it was WSPU policy to stand apart from other political causes, whereas the Federation naturally took an interest in certain issues central to the lives of the working women who were its members, and made many allies among the socialist and labor movements.

In January of 1914, Sylvia was summoned to Paris (where Christabel was in hiding from the police) to meet with her mother and sister, and was there informed that the East London Federation was to be expelled from the WSPU. Christabel argued that working women, because of their poverty and their lack of educational opportunities, were the weakest segment of the women's movement. "We want picked women, the very strongest and most intelligent!" Sylvia quotes her as saying.

The "weak" women in question renamed themselves the East London Federation of the Suffragettes and continued their program of sending speakers into the drawing rooms of society women in Mayfair and Kensington. Among their speakers were **Charlotte Drake,** who had been a barmaid and a sewing machinist; **Melvina Walker,** who had been a lady's maid; Mrs. **Pascoe,** a charwoman who supported her tubercular husband and the orphan child she'd adopted; Mrs. **Schlette,** who was a suffragist in her sixties; **Flora Buchan,** who was fired from her job at a jam factory because of her suffragist activities, and Mrs. **Cressell,** who later became a Borough Councillor.

The East End covers a lot of territory, and the excursions suggested in this chapter—a walk through Whitechapel and Spitalfields, and an outing to Victoria Park—barely begin to explore that territory. Most of the East End does not fall within the traditional tourist area of London. Tube stops are farther apart, busses more infrequent, currency exchange outlets almost nonexistent. These factors make exploring the East End a bit more challenging, but meeting those challenges may lead to one of your most interesting afternoons in London.

Walk One

Begin: Liverpool Street Tube Station
End: Aldgate Tube Station

From the Liverpool Street tube station, follow the exit signs for Old Broad Street, and when you emerge into the daylight you will be standing across from the Liverpool Street train station, itself a spot of historic importance. For the station stands on the site that Bedlam—more properly known as Bethlehem Royal Hospital—once occupied. Bedlam specialized in looking after "distracted people" as early as the fourteenth century. Such caretaking included flogging, cold water dunkings, and being kept chained against the wall. In the seventeenth century the hospital prospered from the donations of the many visitors who came to laugh at the antics of the inmates. (The hospital had by that date been moved to a site in Moorfields.) But in the next century, attitudes toward mental illness began to change, and gradually more humane practices were introduced.

Hannah Snell* (1723–1792) of Wapping was one unhappy inmate who died in Bedlam, although she first led an exciting and eventful life on the outside. Married at age twenty to a Dutch sailor who deserted her, Snell left a baby at home to go in search of her husband. Disguising herself as a boy, she joined the army and marched against the Stuart rebellion in Scotland. According to her autobiography, she received five hundred lashes in Carlisle on a disciplinary charge trumped up by her sergeant because she refused to help him in the criminal seduction of a young woman. After deserting the army she signed up as an assistant cook on a navy vessel bound for East India, and was involved in various battles and shipwrecks before returning to England. She at length discovered that her husband had been executed; she therefore felt at liberty to marry again—twice.

Snell took full advantage of having led an adventurous life: She appeared in uniform upon the stage and later kept a pub in Wapping known as The Female Warrior.

From the station, proceed east along Liverpool Street (passing the Great Eastern Hotel), turn left (north) into Bishopsgate, and right into *Brushfield Street* (by Barclay's Bank). The crates of cucumbers, grapes, melons, and lettuces will assure you that you have reached Spitalfields Market. The present market dates from 1928, but the original fruit and vegetable market on the site was established during the reign of Charles II. In the early eighteenth century the market became the center of the world-famous Spitalfields silks industry. The labor was provided by French Huguenots, the first of many immigrant groups to come to the East End, and the designs were provided by **Anna Maria Garthwaite,** a parson's daughter from Lincolnshire, among others.

If you turn into *Crispin Street*, which comes in on your right, you will see a large structure of brownish-yellow brick with three tiers of hooded windows. This is the Providence Row homeless shelter, founded by the Sisters of Mercy in 1868. The night refuge had 112 beds for women. It is now run by the Providence (Row) Families Association.

Return to Brushfield Street, then turn left into Commercial Street. You are now near the spot where **Mary Kelly,** final victim of Jack the Ripper, was last seen alive. The famous murderer is believed to have been responsible for at least six deaths, and for some months during the year 1888 the East End lay under a siege of terror. His victims were all prostitutes, and they were all murdered in a horribly brutal manner. Their bodies were found with multiple stab wounds, often disembowelled or with their wombs ripped out.

Large sections of the populace, looking for a scapegoat, believed that the murderer must be a Jew, perhaps a "shochet"— a Jewish ritual slaughterer of meat. Anti-Jewish feeling ran high, and there were some incidents of violence. Another rumor claimed that the killer was a Russian anarchist. The truth was never discovered, as the Ripper was never caught; one popular theory today holds that he was a member of the aristocracy.

Turn right into *Hanbury Street,* once the site of the Sugar Loaf public house. At the turn of the century the Sugar Loaf was a gathering place for Jewish anarchists who were involved with the *Arbeter Fraint* movement led by the German Rudolph Rocker. A newspaper article of 1894 said gravely: "The Sugar Loaf, in Hanbury Street, [is one of the] favorite resorts of the East End Anarchists, who get up the weekly discussions that tempt poor flies into the trap. Too lazy to work, they find in the mischievous propaganda they spread a capital means of bringing grist to their own particular mills."

Rose Robins (1885–1971) was often at the Sugar Loaf. "Red" Rose, as she was known, emigrated from Kiev with her parents, travelling in a cattle boat. The conditions were filthy, and the immigrants were fed on salt herring brought around in barrels by a sailor. When she became involved in Rocker's group her parents were appalled: He had been known to lecture on the importance of free love. They tried locking her out of the house one night when she'd been to a meeting as a warning, but she simply left home and moved in with her married sister.

On June 8, 1906, strikers marched through the streets of the

East End, pausing at each tailor's workshop and calling to workers to join them. "Red" Rose was the first one out of her workshop. "I was glad to join the strikers," she said in later years. "My wages then was three shillings and sixpence a day."

Another frequenter of the Sugar Loaf was **Millie Witkop,** who lived in "free union" with Rocker. The two tried to emigrate to New York but were turned away when they refused to go through a marriage ceremony, as they did not believe that love ought to be a matter of law. Millie's sister **Rose Witkop** was a feminist as well as an anarchist; in 1922 she was prosecuted under obscenity laws for publishing *Family Limitations,* Margaret Sanger's work advocating birth control.

Judith Goodman was also part of the *Arbeter Fraint* group that held forth at the Sugar Loaf. Another Russian emigré, Goodman always wore a wig because her hair had been torn out by Cossacks. A socialist revolutionary with strong views about class warfare, she eventually changed her mind about the use of violence, and became a nonviolent agitator in New York City.

Turn right into Brick Lane and you will shortly cross *Princelet Street.* Today you will find yourself among sari shops and are likely to catch the scent of curry in the air, but in 1886 and 1887, Princelet Street was the site of the first Yiddish theater in London, run by Jacob and **Sarah Adler** (1858–1953). It produced plays based on biblical episodes, cast with young men and women of the district. The Adlers eventually moved on to New York City and became celebrated for their work in Yiddish theater, but the tradition they began in the East End continued to thrive for many decades.

Turn right into Fournier Street, which still boasts a number of Georgian buildings. The structure immediately on your right-hand side is emblematic of the changes that Spitalfields has seen over the years. A French Huguenot chapel was built here in 1742—it was one of sixteen in the Spitalfields area—and the site has since been occupied by a Methodist chapel and a synagogue. Today the building serves the Muslim community of the area.

Turn left back into *Commercial Street,* and on your left you will see Christ Church Spitalfields, designed by the famous architect Nicholas Hawksmoor in 1720, and restored in the nineteenth century after being struck by lightning. Over half the names in the graveyard are those of French Huguenots and their descendants. The gardens attached to the church, which used to be much larger, were once known to the homeless who made it their refuge as "Itchy Park." Jack London's *People of the Abyss* (1903) describes his visit to the gardens at three o'clock one afternoon:

> *A chill, raw wind was blowing, and these creatures huddled there in their rags, sleeping for the most part, or trying to sleep. Here were a dozen women, ranging in age from twenty years to seventy. Next a babe, possibly of nine months, lying asleep, flat on the hard bench, with neither pillow nor covering, nor with anyone looking after it. Next half-a-dozen men, sleeping bolt upright or leaning against one another in their sleep. . . . On another bench a woman trimming the frayed strips of her rags with a knife, and another woman, with thread and needle, sewing up rents.*

London notes that as the iron railings prevented people from sleeping there at night, the homeless were obliged to sleep by day.

Christ Church Hall was the site of many strike meetings and radical gatherings. **Annie Besant*** (1847–1933) spoke there frequently during the famous match girls' strike at Bryant and May, in July of 1888. Besant, a socialist and campaigner for birth control, had become incensed by the working conditions at Bryant and May. The factory workers were constantly exposed to yellow phosphorous, still in use twenty years after it became known that the substance resulted in an industrial disease called "phossy jaw" which caused the deterioration of the jawbone. Besant publicized the long hours, poor pay, and hazardous working conditions of the match girls in a series of articles, and was threatened with a libel suit by the match company, Bryant and May. She and fellow socialists distributed leaflets to the women workers as they left the factory. Bryant and May fired three workers as a result of this activity, and on July 5, 1888, 672 women went out on strike. Due to widespread public support generated by Besant's publicity, the match girls won their strike within two weeks. After the successful strike, Besant was elected president of the executive committee of the newly formed Match Makers' Union.

Continue south along Commercial Street toward Whitechapel High Street, and as you approach it you will find Toynbee Hall, the famous settlement house of the East End, on your left. The present building is a postwar replacement of the original structure. Founded by S. A. Barnett in 1884, Toynbee Hall began as a place where university graduates came to live among the poor and working people in the East End while they collected social data and experimented with ways of ameliorating the extreme poverty of the community around them. Associated with Barnett in his work at Toynbee Hall was Dame **Henrietta Octavia Weston Barnett*** (1851–1936). She began working with the reformer Octavia Hill* before her marriage at age twenty-one, and continued her work in public service throughout her life. She helped bring the settlement movement to the United States, raised money for the preservation of eighty acres that are now part of Hampstead Heath, and formed a trust to purchase 240 acres that became the experimental community of Hampstead Garden Suburb (a development with a mix of social classes which also provided a variety of public services). She helped to establish the Metropolitan Association for Befriending Young Servants and to organize afternoon classes for young women who were past school age (over thirteen) but not yet in factories or in service. Today the hall still houses volunteers engaged in social work.

In *Whitechapel High Street*, near its intersection with Commercial Street, is the Whitechapel Art Gallery, which was established in 1901 by Henrietta Barnett, her husband, and others at Toynbee Hall as part of their plan to bring culture to the East End. When she was seventy-two Barnett decided to expand her interest in art; at that time she began painting, and one of her pictures was hung in the Royal Academy.

By now we are in Whitechapel proper, an area made fascinating by the vestiges of the Jewish immigrant community which once dominated the East End. Prices at the famous market in Petticoat Lane (reached via Middlesex Street) are now geared for tourists, but it was once the old clothes exchange of Jewish rag collectors. And crowds pack into Bloom's delicatessen day and evening for their salt beef and potato latkes, though its patrons are as apt to come from the West End as the East. There are shops with mezuzahs on the doorposts, even if many of them have changed the Hebrew lettering on their signs to Bengali.

It's worth noting that Whitechapel was also home to a few members of Britain's one involuntary immigrant group—black slaves. In 1717 a black woman who was the wife of John **Caesar** petitioned the court, claiming that her husband had served Benjamin and John Wood, printers and embossers in Whitechapel, for fourteen years without wages, and had been cruelly treated and sometimes imprisoned. She herself was very poor, and might soon become chargeable to the parish if her husband wasn't allowed to work for wages, she pleaded. One wonders if it was this last argument that convinced the court, which ruled that the Woods must pay Caesar wages, and fixed the amount.

From Commercial Street, turn right (west) on Whitechapel High Street to *Old Castle Street*, and turn right. In the London Polytechnic is housed the fascinating Fawcett Library†, a delight to all researchers of women's history. Enter the Polytechnic by its main doors on the left (west) side of Old Castle Street, go up the stairs to the lobby, turn right, then left when you reach the hall to find the elevator. Take it to the third floor and follow the yellow signs to the Fawcett Library, which will lead you through corridors, up and down stairs, into another elevator, and will deposit you at last in a basement.

The Fawcett Library calls itself the British Museum of the women's movement, and the claim is a just one. It includes about forty thousand books, pamphlets and leaflets, over seven hundred periodical titles, and five hundred boxes of archives, including the personal papers of **Elizabeth Garrett Anderson*** (1836–1917) and **Theresa Billington-Greig*** (1877–1964). In addition to its research facilities, the library has memorabilia from the suffrage movement and sells wonderful postcards which reproduce both portraits of British suffragists and anti-suffrage cartoons.

The library began as the archives of the London Society for

Women's Suffrage, founded in 1867. It was later affiliated with the nonmilitant National Union of Women's Suffrage Societies, founded in 1897 by **Millicent Fawcett*** (1847–1929)—for whom the library is now named—and led by her until women secured the vote in 1918. It was in the 1920s that the collection began to be organized, and in 1926 **Vera Douie** was appointed the first full-time librarian. She stayed on until 1967, and made the Fawcett Library the major research facility it is today. During World War II the library's holdings were evacuated to Oxford—a fortunate move, as the building which had housed it was bombed. In 1977 the library became part of the London Polytechnic.

Return to Whitechapel High Street and turn right, continuing west until it becomes *Aldgate High Street*. (You will pass the Aldgate tube station.) Where Duke's Place and Houndsditch meet you'll find St. Botolph's Church, Aldgate (steps). The original church on this site was one of four London churches dedicated to St. Botolph during the eleventh and twelfth centuries. During the Great Plague over five thousand victims were buried in the churchyard here. The present structure dates back to the eighteenth century, with major changes to the interior in the nineteenth century, but among its most modern furnishings is a statue donated by its sculptor, **Connie Cook,** of the Virgin Mary holding, in her disproportionately large hands, the crown of thorns. The church is active in providing social services for the homeless, including the growing number of homeless women. Female staff and volunteers are available to offer support services, and a women's sitting room is provided during the evenings.

Turn up Duke's Place (by St. John Cass' Foundation Primary School) and follow it until it becomes *Bevis Marks*. The oldest synagogue in London, called the Spanish and Portuguese Synagogue, can be found in a courtyard to your left just past Heneage Lane. The Jews, expelled from England in 1290, returned under Oliver Cromwell in 1657, and the area around the synagogue was settled at that time by Sephardic Jews fleeing the Spanish Inquisition. The present synagogue was built in 1701. Its ornate wood carving and gleaming candelabra show that the community was prospering at the time it was constructed. At the front of the synagogue, on the left-hand side as you face front, is a chair marked with the name of Simon Montefiore, a noted philanthropist and advocate for his people. It was his wife, Lady **Judith Montefiore*** (d. 1862), who endowed a school for rabbis once located in the East End. (The school is still in existence, but has been moved to the West End of London.) Lady Montefiore, of course, sat in the women's gallery, above, and as the synagogue is an Orthodox one, she would sit in the same place today during worship. (Tourists can view the interior of the synagogue only by joining one of the walking tours which explore the area.)

From the synagogue, you can return to the Aldgate tube station, or head north to Bishopsgate and the Liverpool Street tube station where you began.

Walk Two

Begin and End: Bethnal Green Tube Station

If you're blessed with a sunny day in London and you'd like to spend it having a picnic lunch on the grass, Victoria Park may be the perfect alternative to the tourist hordes of Hyde Park. Here you'll find 217 acres of greenery, complete with a fishing pond, a pen of fallow deer, and a refreshment stand. It's a good place to see East End inhabitants at play, and to cap it all off, it holds an honored place in the suffrage history of the early twentieth century.

The occupations practiced by women in Bethnal Green were described in 1861 as those of hawker, sempstress, and prostitute; in 1901 a more official report on the women workers of the Borough of Bethnal Green accounted for 2,275 tailors, 1,516 boot and shoe makers, and 408 French polishers.

From the tube station, located at the edge of the Bethnal Green gardens, follow the signs to the Bethnal Green Museum of Childhood. (If you have children with you, or possibly even if you haven't, you may want to have a look at the museum's dolls, puppets, trains, and board games, some of which date back to the seventeenth century.) Just past the museum turn right onto *Old Ford Road*. To your left you'll see the York Hall Baths, where working women often used the communal laundry in the 1920s. East of the green itself, the Bethnal Green Asylum stood in 1815, and a report made that year observed that "several of the pauper women were chained to their bedsteads naked and covered with only an hempen rug."

Proceed east along Old Ford Road for approximately half a mile, and you'll come to Victoria Park.

The park has long been a debating ground, an assembly point for marches, and the site of public meetings. Women's organizations who used the park included the WSPU, the East London Federation of the Suffragettes (ELFS), the London Match Girls' Union, and the Tailoresses' Union. In October of 1906, an East End crowd was addressed on the suffrage issue by **Hannah Mitchell** (1871–1956). Mitchell, who came from a poor, rural background and had been to school for only two weeks, was a suffragette and a writer and campaigner for the Labour Party.

Annie Kenney* (1879–1953) was another speaker that day. By the time she was thirteen years old, Kenney was working full-time in a Lancashire mill, and she turned early to the labor movement, helping to organize unions in her own and other mills. When she was twenty-six she met the Pankhurst family; she soon became a speaker for the WSPU and eventually became one of the most prominent leaders of the organization, often running it when the Pankhursts were in prison. She herself was arrested and imprisoned many times.

Fanny Goldberg of Whitechapel used to sell the socialist paper *Justice* in Victoria Park. She was a suffragette, campaigned against the suppression of birth control literature, and was a founding member of Great Britain's Communist Party.

If you enter by Crown Gate (East) on the far side of Grove Road, you'll be near the spot where **Sylvia Pankhurst*** suffered one of her more spectacular arrests, on May 24, 1914. The occasion was a "women's May Day," complete with maypoles, to be held in Victoria Park. Sylvia was subject to arrest under the "Cat and Mouse" act, by which suffragettes who endangered their health by hunger strikes in prison were released only long enough to regain their strength before being rearrested. Sylvia marched from the Women's Hall (once at No. 400 Old Ford

Road) to the gates of the park at the center of a chained guard of twenty women. Over fifty plainclothes detectives had penetrated the ranks of the marching crowd by the time they reached the park gates. There the police made a fierce attack on the crowd, dragged the chained guard into the boating enclosure, and locked the gate behind them. They used truncheons to smash the padlocks on the chains. "We received many a blow during the process," Sylvia Pankhurst wrote, "and any woman who attempted to hinder the work had her face pinched, her hair pulled, arms twisted and thumbs bent back, whilst her tormenters gave vent to most lurid epithets." Meanwhile, outside the park gates, police were charging the crowd with horses. Eventually however, the crowd broke down some of the railings and streamed into the park by that means, and the meeting was held as planned. Sylvia Pankhurst, of course, was taken off to prison.

The six-sided pavilion with the pointed roof in the center of the park (east of Grove Road) is the Victoria Fountain, an enormously expensive drinking fountain which was donated by the eccentric heiress **Angela Burdett-Coutts*** (1814–1906). Angela's wealth made her a much sought-after bride, but in her youth she rejected all offers and concentrated on her wealth, which she administrated herself. (She did, according to one story, propose marriage to her friend the Duke of Wellington, when he was seventy-eight and she was thirty-three. He declined gently, and their friendship survived.) She knew everyone who was anyone in the arts and sciences, and was a close personal friend of Dickens. Her most intimate friend, however, was her former governess, Hannah Meredith Brown.

The Victoria Fountain was the least of Angela's philanthropic enterprises, which included educational endowments, model villages, a home for "fallen women," contributions to Florence Nightingale* and Dr. Livingstone, meal tickets for the poor of the East End during its cholera outbreak in 1886, and the unsuccessful Columbia Market in Shoreditch (gone). Baroness Road, in its vicinity, commemorates her contribution, for in 1871 Queen Victoria bestowed a peerage upon her, and she became the first woman in England to be made a baroness in her own right.

Take the diagonal walkway that heads southeast from the fountain and leave the park on its south side, about midway through its eastern sector. You will exit via Gunmakers Lane, which intersects with *Old Ford Road*. Opposite the opening to the lane a pub called the Gunmakers' Arms once stood. It was taken over by ELFS in April 1915, renamed the Mothers' Arms, and used as a day-care center and clinic. Forty children were cared for in the facility, run by **Lucy Burgis**. The clinic, run by Dr. **Alice Johnson,** Dr. **Tchaikovsky,** and Nurse **Hebbes,** also provided lectures in hygiene and nutrition. Hebbes was later the first nurse at the birth control clinic of Marie Stopes*.

Between Gunmakers Lane and Grove Road, on Old Ford Road, the Women's Hall once stood. It opened on May 4, 1914, as the headquarters of the East London Federation of the Suffragettes, though it was also at first the home of Sylvia Pankhurst and several other ELFS leaders. In addition to being a meeting place, the center was used as a milk distribution center and a babies' clinic, and in August of 1914 it was turned into a cost-price restaurant operated by ELFS. Mrs. Ennis **Richmond,** one of the women who ran the kitchen, was much criticized for insisting upon the nutritional value of potato skins.

If you don't fancy walking back to the Bethnal Green tube station, the No. 8 bus will get you back to Central London. To find the bus stop, turn right into Old Ford Road and left immediately into St. Stephen's Road.

5

The Strand and Fleet Street

Begin: Charing Cross Tube Station
End: Chancery Lane Tube Station

"I decided to go to London for the purpose of hearing the Strand roar, which I think one does want, after a day or two of Richmond," Virginia Woolf* wrote in her diary in 1915. Perhaps, but the Strand has roared differently at different times in history. Before the Exeter Exchange was demolished in 1829, one could hear the quite literal roar of lions in the menagerie above the bookstalls; **Mary Lamb*** (1764–1847) heard them often as she walked home along the Strand. Today's roar, of course, is caused by the perpetual automobile traffic, which is like the crash of the ocean in your ear. But the history that hovers amid the theaters, shops, and pubs is worth the din if you can survive it.

In the forecourt of *Charing Cross Station* stands a missilelike memorial to **Eleanor of Castile*** (1244–1290). The present memorial is from the mid-nineteenth century, but the original Eleanor

Cross, erected in 1291 by Edward I, stood for centuries where the statue of Charles I is now, in nearby Trafalgar Square. It was the last of the thirteen crosses the king had erected to mark the resting places of his wife's body as her funeral procession moved from Lincolnshire to Westminster.

Eleanor died while travelling north to join Edward in the Scottish campaigns. Evidently battle did not alarm her; before he came to the throne, she accompanied him on a Crusade, and there is a story that she sucked poison from a wound Edward had received from a poisoned dagger.

Charing Cross was long a bustling center of London activity, and the Golden Door, a toy shop popular in the high society of the 1730s and 1740s, was near here at one time. The shop was operated by the toymaking Chennevix family, including the famous "toywoman of Suffolk Street" **Mary Chennevix.**

The Strand was one of several neighborhoods which were the targets of a massive window-breaking attack staged by militant suffragettes on March 1, 1912. Beginning at 5:30 P.M., in fifteen-minute relays, women broke windows in Downing Street, Regent Street, Oxford Street, Bond Street, the Haymarket, Piccadilly, and the Strand. The following day *The Daily Graphic* reported: "By seven o'clock practically the whole of the West End of London was a city of broken glass. . . . Many of the rioters were young girls, and were terribly nervous when the crucial moment arrived. . . . Between St. Clement Danes and Charing Cross the array of broken windows presented a remarkable spectacle. . . ."

Avoiding broken glass, walk east along the roaring Strand until you come to the *Adelphi Theatre*, a narrow building on the left (north) side of the street just before Adam Street comes in on your right. The theater was one of the grandest in London during the 1890s, in spite of the fact that its stage saw chiefly melodramas. In 1891, the actress always known as Mrs. Pat **Campbell*** (1865–1940) received £7 per week to play the villainess in a melodrama. Stella (she was born Beatrice Rose Stella Tanner) originally began acting in order to support her two children while her first husband, Patrick Campbell, was in Africa prospecting for gold. At the time of her engagement at the Adelphi she was a thin, dark woman almost unknown to London audiences, but she was soon to become one of London's leading ladies.

It was at the Adelphi Theatre in 1899 that **Sarah Bernhardt***
(1844–1923) played Hamlet with great vigor, kicking Polonius in the shins and knocking the heads of Rosencrantz and Guildenstern together. Although in this particular case the critics disapproved of her performance, in general Bernhardt was acknowledged to be one of the greatest and certainly the most fascinating actresses of her day. Theatrical offstage as well as on, she established herself in her rented house in Bayswater with a cheetah, a wolfhound, four dogs, a parrot, and a caged monkey named Darwin. She also had seven chameleons, which she wore (one at a time) on her shoulder to accentuate her dresses. Bernhardt enjoyed male roles in her later years, and at age sixty played the boy lover Pelleas to Mrs. Pat Campbell's Melisande. Further along the Strand you'll pass the intersection of Burleigh Street on your left—that's where those lions roared. Keep pointed toward the church in the middle of the street, and eventually you'll come to a triple archway on the right-hand side of the street which leads into the courtyard of *Somerset House*. The present late eighteenth-century buildings stand on the site of an earlier royal house, where **Anne of Denmark** (1574–1619), queen consort of James I, enjoyed acting in masques written for her by the leading dramatists of the day. This behavior scandalized the Puritan element, which was at this time growing stronger; they felt that the presence of any woman on a stage was highly immoral.

From 1842 to 1848 the Female School of Design, a new division of the Normal School of Design, was housed on the ground floor of Somerset House. The school was attended by middle-class women who wanted to learn a means of supporting themselves, and the students produced designs for carpets, tablecloths, and dress fabrics. It operated under the supervision of the artist **Fanny McIan,** who was so successful in her selection and training of pupils that the instructors of male pupils began to feel threatened by the popularity of the female exhibits. Soon McIan's powers were curtailed, and the school was moved to a less desirable location on the opposite side of the Strand, among the gin palaces and pawnshops. In 1852 the school moved again, to a somewhat better location in Gower Street, but at the same time its fees were almost doubled, and after this it tended to have fewer students whose primary goal was to train for a profession.

There is a long tradition of government offices in Somerset House; it was here that **Mary Ann Talbot*** (1778–1808) came to demand her pension. She had entered the British army disguised as a man, at the persuasion of a man who had seduced her, and was a footboy and later a drummer boy. After her lover's death, she joined the navy as a cabin boy and was wounded at the Battle of Brest, after which she was discharged. She was in time awarded the pension, but it wasn't adequate for her support, and she had much difficulty earning a living. Later she lived with another woman—possibly a lover—and when Talbot was imprisoned for debt, her friend did needlework and laundry in order to meet her prison expenses.

Somerset House now houses certain records and government offices—including the ever-popular Inland Revenue offices—and is also home to the Courtauld Galleries, where you can see *Portrait of the Artist's Sister*, by **Berthe Morisot*** (1841–1895).

Next door to Somerset House are the variegated buildings of *King's College*. A passageway through a sharply modern part of the school leads to some older buildings of dark brick and streaked yellow stone. **Rosalind Franklin** (1920–1958) worked at the Medical Research Council Biophysics Unit of the college. She was the only woman and the only Jew in her department, and she did not get along well with her male colleagues who held many of their scientific discussions in the Common room—a place barred to women. Franklin did significant early work on the microstructure of coal, and later applied X-ray diffraction techniques to the study of the structure of DNA. She was an intimate friend of the Franco-Jewish metallurgist Adrienne Weil, who fled Bordeaux just before German occupation in World War II.

The noted religious writer **Evelyn Underhill** (1875–1941) was made a fellow at King's College in 1927; previously she had lectured on philosophy of religion at Oxford. *Mysticism* (1911) was one of her many titles that made an impact in the field of

Christian spirituality. In 1939, Underhill became a pacifist and wrote the book *The Church and War.*

Leaving King's College, take Melbourne Place north to *Aldwych*, passing between Bush House and Australia House. Turn left into Aldwych and proceed to the foot of Kingsway. From there you will be able to see the massive sculpture high on the Bush House facade (as it faces Kingsway), which is called *Youth.* It was executed by the U.S. sculptor **Malvina Hoffman** (1887–1966), and is dedicated to the friendship of English-speaking peoples. (Ironically, during World War II a flying bomb caused the arm of *America* to fall, killing several people. The arm was replaced in 1977.) Hoffman was commissioned in 1929 to do sculptures of racial types for a *Hall of Man* project; she travelled around the world for two years sculpting people of many different ethnic types in their home environments. She was a close friend of the great dancer Anna Pavlova*, and won a Paris prize in 1911 for her sculpture *Russian Dancers.*

Reverse your course, going east on Aldwych until you reach *Houghton Street*, and turn in for a look at the London School of Economics and Political Science, founded in 1895 by Sidney and **Beatrice Webb*** (1858–1943). Brought up in political and intellectual circles, Beatrice Webb came naturally by her interest in reform. She published research on East End dock life, and in 1888–89 gave evidence before the Lords Commission on the sweating system. While writing *The Cooperative Movement in Great Britain* (1891), she met the Fabian theorist Sidney Webb. They were married the next year and together produced over one hundred books, pamphlets, and articles. During World War I Beatrice wrote the classic: *Wages of Men and Women—Should They Be Equal?*

One student at the school was **Judith Hart*** (b. 1924), who became a Labour M.P. in 1959. She was later Minister of Overseas Development, and wrote *Aid and Liberation: A Socialist Study of Aid Policies* (1973).

Returning to Aldwych, go left, rejoining the Strand. Just west of the Royal Courts of Justice is *Clement's Inn.* Once an Inn of Chancery, it is now devoted to the Mobil Corporation. But in the first years of the twentieth century, **Emmeline Pethick-Law-**

rence* (1867–1954) and her husband lived in a flat here. Emmeline Pethick early became an advocate of women's suffrage and also did social work intended to help working women. When she married Frederick Lawrence in 1901, both of them assumed the hyphenated name Pethick-Lawrence. It was in 1906 that **Christabel Pankhurst*** (1880–1958) came to stay with the Pethick-Lawrences, and for the next six years No. 4 Clement's Inn served as the headquarters of the Women's Social and Political Union, of which Emmeline Pethick-Lawrence was the treasurer and fundraiser. Christabel liked the location: "Adjacent to Fleet Street, it was highly convenient for the newspapers, which were ever interested in the militant movement." Though in their desire for a good story the journalists printed many inaccuracies, Christabel said philosophically, "Even exaggerated and distorted reports, which made us seem more terrible than we really were, told the world this much—that we wanted the vote and were resolved to get it."

Only after the split between the Pankhursts and the Pethick-Lawrences did the WSPU find a new headquarters.

On an island in the middle of the street is the church of St. Clement Danes, by Wren, and in back of it is a statue of Samuel Johnson. On the north side of the statue's base is a relief of Johnson in conversation with a bonneted woman, and the name "Mrs. Thrall" is scratched above it. The woman with the bonnet is really **Hester Thrale*** (1741–1821), of course, intellectual and diarist to whom we owe many anecdotes about Dr. Johnson. Johnson was a great friend of hers and lived with Hester and her first husband for many years. At least, he was a great friend until her second marriage in 1784 to the Italian music teacher Gabriel Piozzi. This marriage so incensed Johnson that he drove the memory of her from his mind (as he told Fanny Burney*), burning all the letters of hers that he could find. As Mrs. Piozzi was very happy in her marriage, it is possible that the sacrifice of cantankerous Dr. Johnson's friendship was endurable. Hester survived Piozzi and lived to celebrate her eightieth birthday by giving a ball for six or seven hundred people at Bath.

Continue along the Strand, passing the Royal Courts of Justice on your left. Just past the courts Bell Yard comes in on the left;

turn right into *Middle Temple Lane* to discover two of London's four Inns of Court—Middle Temple† and Inner Temple†. Parts of some buildings date back to the twelfth century, though far more of it is less than a century old. Still, the atmosphere is unquestionably one of ancient, peaceful, and rigid traditions, and the women who first sought to alter those traditions had no easy task before them.

By the time the first women were called to the Bar in England, women were practicing law in France, Denmark, Finland, Norway, the Netherlands, the Argentine Republic, New Zealand, Russia, all but three states of the United States, parts of Switzerland and Canada, most of Australia, and—if they were unmarried—in Sweden. In the early years of the twentieth century a number of women applied to the various Inns of Court; their applications were uniformly rejected. There had been several court cases testing the legality of those rejections, but judicial opinion held that it was legally impossible for a woman to practice law. Therefore, women turned to a legislative approach, and after much politicking and a war (during which large numbers of women served as clerks in law offices due to the shortage of men), a bill making it legal for women to enter the legal profession became law.

Helena Normanton (1883–1957) was the first woman accepted by the Inns of Court. She had applied to the Middle Temple immediately after women received the vote, but her application was then rejected. On April 11, 1919, which was Ladies' Night of the Union Society of the Middle Temple, Normanton spoke in favor of women entering the legal profession. Those present included the Indian law student **Cornelia Sorabji** (1866–1954), who later became the first woman in India to practice law. In December of that year the Sex Disqualification (Removal) Bill became law, and on January 11, 1920, women students in robes dined in the Middle Temple Hall for the first time in its long history.

The first woman called to the Bar in England (six months after the first woman had been called to the Irish bar) was Dr. **Ivy Williams** (1877–1966), a member of the Inner Temple. Williams already held an advanced degree in law, and was a tutor and lecturer in the subject to the Society of Oxford Home Students, a position which she continued to hold until 1945. Though called to the Bar in May of 1922, in fact she never practiced, as she preferred an academic career. When she discovered later in life that her eyesight was failing, she became an authority on Braille, writing a primer and teaching blind students from all over the country. Williams also endowed two law scholarships at Oxford, one of them open to women only.

Normanton was the second woman in England to be called to the Bar and the first to practice law. She did not abandon her feminism because she'd reached her goal; she retained her name after marriage, and her works include *Sex Differentiation in Salary* and *Everyday Law for Women*.

The first woman judge in England, **Elizabeth Kathleen Lane** (1905–1988) became a barrister at the Inner Temple at age thirty-five. When she was appointed to the Bench, reporters plied her with such questions as "Does needlework help you relax?" and "What feminine qualities can you bring to the Bench?" Lane smiled politely as she reprimanded: "That is too personal."

The Temple Church is shared by the Inner and Middle Temples. As you enter you will see a picture of the church after it was bombed in 1941; it was done by **Kathleen Allen** (1906–1983), one of a number of artists appointed to record the effects of the bombing on London. Allen studied at the Royal College of Art. Her works include many industrial subjects.

Returning to *Fleet Street*, turn right and cross to the north side of the street, then continue east until you reach the modern glass and concrete building of Coutts & Co. A group of women writers used to meet regularly at this address in the 1890s. Around 1900 **Honnor Morten,** a member of the school board and author of several books on nursing and midwifery, accepted a dare from fellow members and walked the length of Fleet Street smoking a cigarette—unthinkable behavior for a woman in those days. Unfortunately, she encountered on her walk a straight-laced man who was one of her most influential constituents. She shortly lost her place on the board as a representative of Hackney; however, she was able to represent Southwark instead. As a school board member she campaigned against corporal punishment and for equal pay.

Next door you will see St. Dunstan's in the West (where the playwright **Catherine Trotter's*** husband was once curate). To the right of the church is a bust of the newspaper magnate Lord Northcliffe, done by Lady **Kathleen Kennet*** (1878–1947). As Kathleen Bruce, she studied at the Slade School of Art and then at Colarossi's studios in Paris. Her marriage to Hilton Young, later Lord Kennet, in 1922, was her second; she had previously been married to the Polar explorer Captain Robert Scott. To the right of Kennet's bust is a statue of Queen **Elizabeth I*** (1533–1603), which was on Lud Gate until that City Gate was taken down in 1760.

It was on Fleet Street near St. Dunstan in the West that the silversmith Mrs. **Pagitter** had her shop at the beginning of the eighteenth century.

Fleet Street was the home for a time of **Katherine Philips** (1631–1664), who lived here after her marriage. Philips founded a "Society of Friendship" which was a kind of correspondence club in which each writer adopted a pseudonym. She herself was known as "the Matchless Orinda." Her passionate verses to Anne Owen would certainly be considered lesbian love poems if published today, but it may be that her passion excluded physical expression.

From St. Dunstan, retrace your steps on Fleet Street until you reach *Chancery Lane*, then turn right. Where the Public Records Office now stands, a "Domus Conversorum" stood in medieval times, that is, a royal home for converted Jews. The institution was founded by Henry III in 1232, and was used by many destitute Jews who had no other means to support themselves. Here they lived at the expense of the Crown—that is to say they were supported by moneys the Crown had confiscated from other Jews. Whole families lived in the Conversorum, and the names of a number of women are known, including that of **Christiana of Oxford** and of **Isabella,** who received a special gift of a tunic of russet brown cloth from the Crown.

At the northern end of Chancery Lane turn right into Holborn, and in a short distance you will find the Chancery Lane tube station.

6

Covent Garden

Begin: Covent Garden Tube Station
End: Leicester Square Tube Station

Covent Garden is still dominated by the vast, airy Covent Garden Market, though it no longer sells flowers and vegetables. Today it's a shopping center, with every manner of shop competing for the tourist pound (or dollar), and frequent noontime shows by enterprising musicians who perform in the piazza. But the streets which surround the market—streets like Garrick, Kemble, and Kean—remind one that Covent Garden is above all a theater district, both historically and today.

If you turn right (roughly east) into *Long Acre* from the tube station, you will be near the site where the actress and writer **Charlotte Charke*** (1710?–1760), the youngest daughter of the playwright Colley Cibber, was once a grocer and oil dealer. This was just one phase of Charke's colorful career. From a child she was more fond of grooming horses and digging in the garden than of needlework, and she later adopted male dress and acted exclusively in male roles. Her book *A Narrative of the Life of Mrs. Charlotte Charke, Written by Herself*, which was published in 1755, bragged about her sexual successes with women who were unable to see past her masculine disguise. Always on the edge of poverty, Charke set up a puppet show, sold sausages, was a waiter, and even became a valet to a nobleman (masquerading as a man, of course) in order to support her child. Once she was sent to a "sponging-house"—a kind of preliminary debtors' prison—but the coffeehouse keepers of Covent Garden and their female frequenters took up a collection for her release.

At No. 100 Long Acre **Emma Martin***, a midwife, kept a surgical bandage shop in the late 1840s, where among her stock she sold products that were probably contraceptives. She wrote a number of tracts, some of which argued that female health care should be the province of females, and gave lectures on topics such as "Gestation" or "Abortion: Its Prevention."

Continue down Long Acre until, as it crosses Drury Lane, it becomes *Great Queen Street*. Just past Wild Street you will find the Freemasons' Hall, a large building in the classical style flanked by imposing columns and three-branched lamps. In 1840 the World Anti-Slavery Convention was held in the original hall on this site. Though the gathering lasted several days and many fine speeches were made there, it is best remembered by many for its handling of "the woman question"—the question of whether or not female delegates from the United States should be seated on the convention floor. On the first day of the convention the women delegates were made to sit in the gallery with other spectators—including British women **Amelia Opie** (1769–1853), the Quaker devotional poet and former novelist, and Lady **Noel Byron*** (1792–1860), the educational reformer. Meanwhile, on the convention floor, the debate about whether or not to seat them raged. In the end, the women were denied their seats, and two of the ousted delegates—**Lucretia Mott*** (1793–1880) and **Elizabeth Cady Stanton** (1815–1902)—were so furious that they went home and called the first women's rights convention in the United States, held in Seneca Falls in 1848.

The Anti-Slavery Convention influenced British women as well. Observer **Anne Knight** afterward helped to found the Sheffield Female Political Association, which issued a manifesto in favor of votes for women in 1851.

Across the street from the Freemasons' Hall, a federation of small unions called the Women's Protective and Provident League once had its headquarters. Composed of dressmakers, upholsterers, bookbinders, artificial flower makers, and similar workers, it was founded in 1874 by **Emma Patterson** (1848–1886). The League offered a library, a savings bank, and a swimming club to its members and organized inexpensive holiday excursions.

Retrace your steps to Long Acre, turning left at the International Herald Tribune building into *Bow Street*. In a short distance you'll find the Bow Street Magistrates' Court, on the left-hand side of the street—you'll see the lion and unicorn over the window. It was here that the militant suffragettes were often brought for their misdeeds. On January 7, 1908, **Flora Drummond*** (1869–1940) appeared here. Drummond was a small, stout Scotswoman, known as "the general" because she often led London suffragette marches with a drum and fife. She was so short that although she had trained as a telegraphist early in her life, the post office disqualified her from the work due to her stature. Drummond was brought here after having been arrested at No. 10 Downing Street, where she had actually managed to enter the premises. She was sent to prison for three weeks after she refused to be bound over to keep the peace.

Ten years later, the Bow Street Magistrates' Court saw the sensational obscenity trial held on the book *The Well of Loneliness*. The novel's author was **Marguerite Radclyffe Hall*** (1883–1943), known to her friends as "John." John used her book to plead for tolerance of lesbianism, or "inversion," as she called it. Though many lesbians—then and now—have found the book objectionable due to its stereotyping, there's no doubt that Hall's courage in writing and defending her novel radically altered public awareness of lesbianism. She received hundreds of letters of support and gratitude from women throughout Britain.

The trial was held on November 9, 1928, in a room that was crowded to capacity several hours before the court convened. Most of the spectators were women. John was there, wearing a dark blue Spanish riding hat and a leather motor-coat. The fact that she was not allowed to take the witness stand galled her

Radclyffe Hall

extremely; she wanted to declare that she was not ashamed of herself, her life, or her book. But at that time the law held only the publisher and distributors, not the author, accountable in obscenity trials, and the defense strategy did not include putting John on the stand. Instead, forty defense witnesses were prepared to testify that day, including Virginia Woolf*—though she had uncomfortable doubts about the book's literary merit. However, the magistrate disallowed "opinions" as evidence and decided to come to an independent conclusion about the contents of *The Well of Loneliness*. The novel, by the way, contains no obscene words and no sex scenes, and its most scandalous phrase—"and that night they were not divided"—has biblical origins.

The magistrate's verdict was delivered to another packed courtroom at Bow Street on November 16. He found it obscene on the grounds that it defended "acts of the most horrible, unnatural and disgusting obscenity," and women "living in filthy sin." John and the many other women in the room who regularly engaged in such "acts" listened in fury.

The Well of Loneliness was published in many other countries—including the United States—and in several languages, including Dutch, French, and Italian. But it wasn't republished in Britain until 1949, six years after the death of Radclyffe Hall.

An interesting aside: John had been a Conservative all her life, but at the time of the trial she was impressed to find that it was from Labour that she received some support. The National Union of Railwaymen and the South Wales Miners' Federation both sent signed protests against the government seizure of her books. A few months later, when the miners were on strike and low on funds, John sold one of her most treasured possessions— a portrait, by John Singer Sargent, of her deceased lover Mabel Batten—and donated the money to the Lord Mayor of London's Fund for the Relief of Distress in the Coalfields.

Almost immediately opposite the police court is the Royal Opera House, which surprisingly enough has associations with suffragette history. In December 1913, at a gala performance of *Jeanne d'Arc* attended by the king and queen, the suffragettes obtained a box directly opposite the Royal Box. It was occupied by three lavishly gowned women who, after entering, locked and barricaded the door behind them. After the close of the first act, one of the women stood and addressed the king with a megaphone, pointing out that the suffragettes were fighting for liberty, just as Joan of Arc had. She continued speaking, in spite of the consternation of the audience and authorities, until the door to the box was broken down and the women were ejected.

At this moment, about forty women in the gallery dropped armloads of suffrage literature onto the heads of those below. All in all, it was forty-five minutes before the opera could be resumed.

The Opera House also has a more theatrical set of women associated with it. A theater has existed on this site since 1732, and many brilliant actresses appeared at what was known as the Covent Garden Theatre. **Peg Woffington*** (1714–1760) dominated its stage from 1754–57. **Frances Abington** (1737–1815), who was as famous for her sexual exploits as for her dramatic ability, came here in 1782 after quarrelling with the management at Drury Lane and continued to work into her sixties. The musical **Elizabeth Billington** (1768–1818) sang here in 1786 and was such an outstanding success that she was immediately engaged for the entire season. Billington, the illegitimate daughter of an oboist from the King's Theatre, was trained by her father and composed two piano sonatas before she was twelve. Her musical career was more successful than her love life: She was accused by her enemies of having caused the sudden death of her first husband, and her own death may have been caused by a blow received from her second.

In 1797 the actress **Julia Betterton Glover*** (1779–1850) made her debut here, playing Elwina in the play *Percy* by **Hannah More*** (1745–1833). More came from an intellectual family, and was taught Latin and math as a child until her superior ability alarmed her father, who feared she would grow unfeminine. The lessons stopped, but More continued. When she first arrived in London she grew very involved with the world of the theater, and wrote several successful plays, but shortly her religious experiences led her to devote herself to "good works," including teaching miners' children and attempting to quell labor unrest through the distribution of religious literature.

The theater has also seen some dramatic farewell performances, most notably that of **Sarah Siddons*** (1755–1831), who retired from the stage in 1812. Two years later **Dorothy Jordan*** (1762–1816) performed for the last time, playing Lady Teazle in Richard Brinsley Sheridan's *School for Scandal*, a role for which she was famous. Jordan's acting career was periodically interrupted by pregnancy, as she was the mistress of the Duke of Clarence, later King William IV; she bore him ten children in the twenty years they lived together. In 1811 he ended their relationship in order to give England a queen; in 1814 she retired from the stage; in 1816 she died at St. Cloud, suffering from mental delusions.

It was in Bow Street that Will's Coffee House stood in Restoration London. It was patronized by the playwright **Aphra Behn*** (1640?–1689), as well as by other literary wits.

From Bow Street turn left into Russell Street, and you will come almost immediately to Theatre Royal, Drury Lane, which actually fronts on *Catherine Street*. The present building dates from 1812, with the portico added in 1820 and the colonnade in 1831. But the first theater on the site opened in 1663. During the Commonwealth, the Puritans had effectively banned theater as a frivolous and immoral entertainment, but with the return of Charles II to the throne all that changed; no one was more frivolous than he. Suddenly the boards abounded with actresses, most of whom lived up to their reputations as loose-living women. It was so much the custom for wealthy men to choose their mistresses from among the players that some women begged for the opportunity to go on stage simply for the chance of finding a suitable protector. So it was that **Nell Gwynne*** (1650–1687), who made her debut at Drury Lane in 1665 in Dryden's *Indian Emperor*, was discovered by Charles II himself, and "pretty, witty Nell" became one of his favorite mistresses.

With the actress **Elizabeth Barry*** (1658–1713) the situation was reversed; her protector, the Earl of Rochester, functioned as her drama coach. He encouraged her to feel genuinely the emotions she was portraying, and she learned her lesson so well that English audiences grew enamored of her. A contemporary critic said of her that she was "the finest woman in the world upon the stage, and the ugliest woman off on't," a reference to the fact that she was considered plain. Barry was said to be promiscuous, rapacious, and bad tempered. On one occasion she quarrelled with another actress, **Betty Boutel**, just before the play began, and when Barry came to the line: "Die, sorceress, die, and all my wrongs die with thee!" she went at Mrs. Boutel so energetically that her blunted stage dagger drove through Boutel's stays and actually pierced her flesh.

In 1695, Drury Lane produced a play called *Agnes de Castro*, written by sixteen-year-old **Catherine Trotter*** (1679–1749), later Catherine Cockburn. (The play was a dramatization of a short story by Aphra Behn*.) This precocious playwright seemed destined for a long and successful career, but after writing four plays she turned to theology and philosophy as subjects. On one occasion, someone expressed doubt that the ideas in her philosophical works were her own. Trotter defended herself with spirit, writing:

> *Women are as capable of penetrating into the grounds of things and reasoning justly as men are who certainly have no advantage of us but in their opportunities of knowledge . . . when anything is written by a woman that they cannot deny their approbation to, [men] are sure to rob us of the glory of it by concluding 'tis not her own.*

The year 1696 was a good year for women playwrights; in addition to Trotter's play, the Drury Lane company produced a comedy of intrigue called *The Spanish Wives*, by **Mary Pix*** (1666–before 1709), and *The Lost Lover, or: The Jealous Husband*, by **Mary Delariviere Manley*** (1663–1724). They also produced *Oroonoko*, which was a dramatization by Thomas Southerne of a novel by the same title published by **Aphra Behn*** in 1687. Inspired by her life in Surinam, the novel tells the story of an African prince who has been sold into slavery and anticipates the abolitionist movement by many years.

A few years later, Drury Lane began producing the comedies of **Susannah Centlivre*** (d. 1723), including *The Perjured Husband* (1700), which was much criticized for indecent language, and *The Busy Body* (1709), an extraordinarily popular play which was performed regularly through the nineteenth century. A half century after that, in 1763, the theater produced two plays by **Frances Sheridan*** (1724–1766), mother of the more famous Richard Brinsley Sheridan. One was called *The Discovery* and one *The Dupe*.

Drury Lane has been the home of many great actresses (and more obscure ones). The famous **Anne Oldfield*** (1683–1730), renowned for her beauty and for her ability to play both tragedy and comedy, had many theatrical triumphs here, and here **Charlotte Charke*** played Roderigo in *Othello*. **Peg Woffington***, who was unusually tall and had a harsh voice, was famous for her "breeches" roles. She played Sir Harry Wildair in *The Constant Couple* with such success that she once received an insistent proposal of marriage from a woman afterward. Presumably, she wasn't interested, since she was famous for her sexual liaisons with men.

The great **Sarah Siddons*** made her debut here in 1775, playing Portia in *The Merchant of Venice*. Siddons was born into the theatrical Kemble family, and in childhood played parts in her father's touring company. Her London debut, which she made at age twenty, was not a success, but after some polishing in the provinces, she returned to mesmerize audiences with her intense tragic roles and rapidly became the idol of London.

In 1779, **Mary "Perdita" Robinson** (1758–1800) played Perdita in *The Winter's Tale* and was discovered by the Prince of Wales (later George IV), but he abandoned her after two years. In 1791 it was the Duke of Clarence, later William IV, who discovered **Dorothy Jordan***.

In the early nineteenth century, **Julia Betterton Glover*** was a member of the Drury Lane company. She left her husband when she found he was supporting a mistress with her money, but he sued for her earnings and won. He also tried to get custody of their children, but she managed to keep them, if not the money to raise them.

On June 12, 1906, **Ellen Terry*** (1847–1928) held a mammoth matinee at Drury Lane to celebrate her Jubilee—fifty years on the stage. Many members of her very theatrical family, including siblings, offspring, nieces, and nephews, participated in the show—but her two-year-old grandnephew, now Sir John Gielgud, stayed home. A few years later, Terry began acting only on rare occasions and concentrated instead upon writing, lecturing, and doing readings from Shakespeare. Terry had three marriages, none of them successful, but she always called Shakespeare her true sweetheart. "Wonderful women!" she said in a lecture called "The Triumphant Women," given in 1911.

"Have you ever thought how much we all, and women especially, owe to Shakespeare for his vindication of women in these fearless, high-spirited, resolute and intelligent heroines?"

Leaving Drury Lane, retrace your steps down *Russell Street*. It was in the southwest portion of the street that **Elizabeth Inchbald*** (1753–1821) lived in 1788, when she wrote the play *Such Things Are*. Pass through the great glass and stone shopping center of Covent Garden (ramp), once the fruit and flower market where Eliza Doolittle met Henry Higgins. (The role of Eliza, which is originally from George Bernard Shaw's *Pygmalion*, was created by him for Mrs. Pat Campbell*.) Emerge on the south side of the market and jog left into *Henrietta Street*. Here **Hannah More*** stayed in 1774, on her first visit to London. Later on she became acquainted with the women in the Bluestocking set and began to write plays. One of England's finest novelists, **Jane Austen*** (1775–1817), stayed with her brother at No. 10 in 1813—the same year that *Pride and Prejudice* was published. Austen had actually written the lively work sixteen years earlier, when she was twenty-one. Austen's indirect commentaries upon the moral implications of social relations are still pertinent today, and her deftly drawn characters and humorous irony make her one of the most readable novelists of any time period.

At the west end of Henrietta Street, turn right into *Bedford Street*, and before long you'll see the entrance to the charming churchyard of St. Paul's, Covent Garden, known as "the actors' church." In this red brick church (stairs) Lady **Mary Wortley Montagu*** (1689–1762) was baptized in 1689. Though her lively letters were her most famous writings, Montagu was most probably also the author of the spirited essay *Woman Not Inferior to Man*.

Though most of the plaques that you'll see inside the church are dedicated to modern performers, the theatrical tradition of the church is very old: The playwright **Susannah Centlivre*** was buried there in 1723. The church contains a casket holding the ashes of **Ellen Terry***, and plaques to **Vivien Leigh** (1913–1967), to the music hall artist **Marie Lloyd** (1870–1922), and to **Lilian Baylis** (1874–1937), who is known for her management of the

"Old Vic" theater and her inauguration of magnificent Shakespearean productions there. Among the other memorial plaques you'll find the names of many women who have contributed as performers, choreographers, and designers to the theatrical arts.

When you've paid your tribute to the dramatic dead, veer left into Garrick Street from the north end of Bedford Street, then turn left again at Cranbourne to find the Leicester Square tube station.

7

Trafalgar Square

Begin and End: Charing Cross Tube Station

Trafalgar Square is the home of the high-rise statue of Admiral Nelson. It's also the home of the four Landseer lions who guard the statue's base, of two fountains, fifty vendors who specialize in birdseed, two thousand tourists, and four thousand pigeons (numbers approximate). The square is bounded on all sides by rushing traffic—it's a good place to catch a bus if you have some idea of what to do with it once you've caught it. If you'd rather leave by tube, Charing Cross, in the Strand, is closest, though the Leicester Square tube station, a few blocks north on Charing Cross Road, is also very handy.

Before going into the history of the square proper, it's interesting to have a look at a few key buildings which lie beyond the traffic moat. To the north is the very grand National Gallery†, which houses an immense collection of paintings done between the thirteenth and nineteenth centuries. All but a handful of these are by men, of course, but the collection does include some rarely seen works by early women artists. Whether or not these works will be on display is problematical. If you are seriously

97

interested in viewing a particular painting, your best bet is to make prior arrangements.

One of the works in the National Gallery's collection is a lively painting called *A Boy and a Girl With a Cat and an Eel*, by the Dutch painter **Judith Leyster** (1609–1660). Leyster was the daughter of a brewer and spent most of her life in Amsterdam; she entered the Haarlem Guild of St. Luke in 1633. She was apparently a thorough-going professional, as she once sued the painter Frans Hals for luring one of her students into his studio without giving Leyster any compensation.

Several works by **Katharine de Hemessen** (1527–after 1587) can be seen in the National Gallery. She was also a Dutch painter and trained in her father's studio. But her half-length portraits and small religious works use a simpler and more subdued style than those of Jan Sanders de Hemessen. Only ten signed and dated pictures of hers have been found, all dated previous to her marriage in 1554. She may have quit working at that time.

The eighteenth-century Italian miniaturist **Rosalba Carriera** (1657–1757) followed her mother's trade of lace making in her early life, but eventually turned to decorating snuff boxes for Venetian tourists, and by the year 1700 she was selling minia-tures. She was one of the originators of the rococo style in Italy and France, and was elected to the Academy of Rome in 1705.

Two works by the Parisian painter **Elizabeth Louise Vigée-Le Brun** (1755–1842) are part of the collection of the National Gal-lery, one of them a self-portrait. Le Brun was a fashionable portrait painter, patronized by Marie Antoinette*, among others. In addition to being an accomplished painter, she also wrote a book of memoirs.

The gallery also houses a version of French painter **Rosa Bonheur's** famous painting, *The Horse Fair.* Bonheur (1822–1899) loved to paint animals; she obtained body parts from the butcher in order to study their anatomy, and regularly visited the cattle markets. To avoid attracting attention, she dressed as a boy on these expeditions. (In fact, she dressed in men's clothing all her life, donning skirts only for very formal occasions.) In 1841 Bonheur exhibited at the Paris Salon, and in 1849 she took over her father's position as director of l'Ecole Imperiale de Dessin, where her sister was also an instructor. In 1853 she bought an estate near Fountainbleau and lived there for forty years with her intimate friend Nathalie Micas, also a painter. The full-scale version of *The Horse Fair* is in the New York Metropolitan Museum. The painting which is owned by the National Gallery was probably begun by Micas and finished by Bonheur.

Summer's Day, a painting by the French impressionist **Berthe Morisot*** (1841–1895), can also be seen at the National Gallery. Morisot was the daughter of a respectable bourgeois, and as such began taking drawing lessons when she was fifteen. But her interest in art, and her ambition, went far beyond what was seemly for a woman of her class. She studied with Corot and exhibited at the Paris Salon of 1864. But it was her association with Edouard Manet that taught her most about painting, and incidentally, also influenced Manet's style. After her marriage to Edouard's brother Eugene in 1874, she exhibited in the first impressionist show and was thereafter deeply involved in the impressionist movement.

Around the corner from the National Gallery, in Charing Cross Road, you will find the National Portrait Gallery†, where you will be able to view the faces of many of the women who have appeared in other chapters of this book. The museum is arranged chronologically, so that you can work your way through the centuries, admiring the women of yesteryear. Hundreds of portraits of British women are contained in the museum's vast collection (though not all works are on display at any one time).

You will want to be leisurely in your perusal of the galleries, and by no means limit yourself to the portraits mentioned below. Queens and royal mistresses are well represented from the outset, of course, as are ladies of the nobility. Be sure to see the striking portrait of Queen **Elizabeth I*** (1533–1603) which depicts her standing regally upon a map of England. Lady **Jane Grey*** (1537–1554), who was "queen" for nine days, is shown, and there is an interesting portrait of Lady **Margaret Beaufort*** (1443–1509) which shows her in a white wimple, holding a book of devotions in her hand. Lady Margaret translated many devotional works, encouraged the first printing presses, endowed two Cambridge colleges, and founded several professorships.

Literary women are so well represented in the collection of the National Portrait Gallery that it would be impractical to name more than a few. In addition to all the literary lionesses in Britain's past—including **George Eliot***, the **Brontë*** sisters, **Jane Austen***, and **Elizabeth Barrett Browning***—there are portraits of women of letters such as **Jane Welsh Carlyle***, Lady **Mary Wortley Montagu***, and **Fanny Burney***. In a case near the portrait of **Mary Shelley*** there is a copy of an early edition of her novel, *Frankenstein*.

One early woman of letters was **Dorothy Osborne*** (1627–1695), whose portrait can be found among the Stuarts. Dorothy was an intelligent young woman from a Royalist family who lived during the Commonwealth period. Forbidden to marry the man of her choice, she carried on a lively correspondence with him over the course of several years, until they were at last permitted to become engaged. Her letters are a valuable source of information about daily life among the aristocracy during this period. Sensitive and moody, but capable of poking fun at herself, Dorothy wrote to her intended after they became engaged: "You are like to have an excellent housewife of me; I am abed still, and slept so soundly, nothing but your letter could have waked me."

More recent literary women represented in the collection include **Virginia Woolf*** (1882–1941) by Duncan Grant, the eccentric poet **Edith Sitwell*** (1877–1964), and **Radclyffe Hall*** (1883–1943), author of the notorious lesbian novel, *The Well of Loneliness*. The painting was donated by her lover, Lady Una Troubridge. **Iris Murdoch** (b. 1919) is also represented in the National Portrait Gallery. Murdoch, whose training was in philosophy, is the author of many compelling novels which explore the presence of evil and power of love in contemporary life.

A goodly number of reformers are pictured in the Gallery, including **Elizabeth Fry*** (1780–1845) and **Octavia Hill*** (1838–1912), and a scattering of feminists—such as **Barbara Bodichon*** (1827–1891) and **Charlotte Despard*** (1844–1939)—are included in the collection. There are also pictures of political women like

Nancy Astor* (1879–1964) and **Margaret Bondfield*** (1873–1953).

A number of women artists have dual representation in the Gallery's collection; both their faces and their works appear. The Restoration portraitist **Mary Beale*** (1623–1699) is the earliest of these. Her self-portrait was done in 1687. The painters **Angelica Kauffmann*** (1741–1807), **Gwen John*** (1876–1939), and **Laura Knight*** (1877–1970) have all done self-portraits which now belong to the National Portrait Gallery; Knight's shows her painting, with a nude model before her. Some of the photographs in the Gallery—including several shots of Thomas Carlyle—were taken by the pioneer photographer **Julia Margaret Cameron** (1815–1879).

In addition to painters, the work of at least one woman sculptor is part of the Gallery's holdings. There is a bust of the comedienne **Elizabeth Farren** (1759?–1829)—later Countess of Derby—by **Anne Seymour Damer** (1749–1828). Lord Derby was probably not enthusiastic about the piece; he alleged that Damer's interest in the woman who was then his mistress was not wholly an artistic one, and accused the sculptor of "liking her own sex in a criminal way." Damer's sculptural subjects included Napoleon and Lord Nelson.

When you have satisfied your hunger for female faces from history, you will find the beautiful church of St. Martin's-in-the-Fields just northeast of Trafalgar Square. It was here that **Nell Gwynne*** (1650–1687), one of Charles II's many mistresses, was buried in the churchyard in 1687. (You can see her portrait by Lely at the National Portrait Gallery.)

On the island in St. Martin's Place stands an imposing statue of **Edith Cavell*** (1865–1915), which glitters white against the gray of the patriotic monument behind it. In 1907 Cavell, who had taken her nurse's training at London Hospital, was appointed Head of Nursing at Belgium's first training school for nurses, the Birkendael Medical Institute in Brussels. When the Germans invaded Belgium the school became a Red Cross hospital, where all wounded, regardless of nationality, were treated. But it also became a resting point for French and British soldiers en route to the Netherlands, and Cavell was active in smuggling out allied soldiers. She was apprehended by the Germans in August of 1915, and was executed by a firing squad on October 12, 1915. Cavell's words have become famous: "Patriotism is not enough. I must have no hatred or bitterness toward anyone."

Due east of Trafalgar Square is South Africa House, very handy for the anti-apartheid demonstrations held at the square. But these are not the only protestors to make use of this time-honored rallying point. The square, which holds about fifty thousand, has been used by Communists, trade unionists, neo-fascists, religious sects, feminists—and of course, suffragettes—to express their fierce displeasure with the status quo.

Trafalgar Square became part of suffragette history at 3 P.M. on May 19, 1906. In the words of **Sylvia Pankhurst***: "On this ground, consecrate to the discontented and oppressed, under that tall column topped by the statue of the fighting Nelson and on that wide plinth, flanked by the four crouching lions, the first big open-air women's suffrage meeting was held." Seven thousand people attended, and the speakers, who stood between those same lions you see today, included Mrs. **Westenholme-Elmy,** whose long gray curls were a reminder of the many years of work she put into the "old" suffragist movement; **Annie Kenney*** (1879–1953), the mill worker from Lancashire; **Theresa Billington** (later Billington-Greig*) (1877–1964), who later broke with the Pankhursts over the use of violence and over the single-issue orientation of their movement; and of course, Sylvia's mother, **Emmeline Pankhurst*** (1858–1928). It was the first of many such meetings.

Five years later, on April 2, 1911, suffragettes used Trafalgar Square in a rather different way. It was the day of the census, and feminists were protesting their lack of citizenship by staying away from home during all of the twenty-four hour period during which the census was taken. Women walked about Trafalgar Square until midnight, at which time they went to the Aldwych skating rink, where they enjoyed themselves until morning.

By the time another five years had passed, the suffragette movement had become badly divided. During World War I, the

Women's Social and Political Union, led by Emmeline Pankhurst, gave strong support to the war effort, ceased its efforts toward enfranchisement, and concentrated its energies on trying to obtain significant responsibilities for women doing war work. But Sylvia Pankhurst decried the war and its effect on women, particularly working women in the East End of London. On April 8, 1916, she led an antiwar delegation from the East End to Trafalgar Square to demand "human suffrage and no infringement of popular liberties." Upon hearing of this gathering, Emmeline Pankhurst cabled from the United States, where she was lecturing, "Strongly repudiate and condemn Sylvia's foolish and unpatriotic conduct. Regret I cannot prevent use of name. Make this public."

The Pankhursts never resolved their family differences, but women in England secured the vote regardless. However, the struggle for full equality is far from over, and those who pass by Trafalgar Square should not be surprised if they find themselves witnessing yet one more protest in favor of women's rights—not completely unlike the one first issued there over eighty years ago.

8

Soho and Fitzrovia

Begin: Piccadilly Circus Tube Station
End: Warren Street Tube Station

Soho, the neighborhood north of Trafalgar Square, is a fascinating and sometimes slightly sleazy area filled with pubs, postcards, peep shows, foreign food markets, and ethnic eateries. Though the earliest residents of the district were aristocrats, by the end of the seventeenth century it was already acquiring a reputation for having many foreigners, the first of these being French Huguenots. In the mid-nineteenth century Soho became noted for its theaters, music halls, and brothels, and somewhat later for its excellent foreign restaurants, including many Greek and Italian establishments. Today the area is home to London's Chinatown.

From the Piccadilly Circus tube station, go around the north side of the circus and head north on Glasshouse, then veer almost at once into Sherwood Street. This will lead you to *Golden Square*, which will probably seem lovely and peaceful after the rush of traffic on Piccadilly. In the late eighteenth century, when the square was dominated by foreign legations and painters, the

Swiss painter **Angelica Kauffmann*** (1741–1807) lived in No. 16—now a bookshop—on the south side of the square. Kauffmann, one of the founding members of the Royal Academy, was a friend of the painters Sir Joshua Reynolds and Henry Fuseli. In fact, the latter fell in love with her, but Kauffmann preferred the attentions of a Count de Horn, and she married him in 1767. He turned out to be an adventurer, already married, and no count. Kauffmann was publicly humiliated, but it didn't seem to affect the extreme popularity of her work. She later married the Italian painter Antonio Zucchi.

In No. 19, at a somewhat earlier date, lived Lady **Mary Wortley Montagu*** (1689–1762). This remarkable, self-educated woman carried on correspondences with Mary Astell* and, almost passionately, with Anne Wortley Montagu, whose brother she later married in a romantic elopement. The marriage, however, was not a success, and in later years she spoke cynically of matrimony. In advising her granddaughter not to marry, she wrote: "In a lottery where there are (at the lowest computation) ten thousand blanks to a prize, it is the most prudent choice not to venture."

Both of these houses in Golden Square have been rebuilt.

Retrace your steps and head toward the easternmost point of Piccadilly Circus, where you'll turn right into *Haymarket* and proceed south. Take a glance to the right as you pass *Norris Street*, where, in 1731 **Elizabeth Godfrey** (then Buteaux) was a silversmith in this street, having taken over the business of her husband upon his death. Her mark was EB on a diamond-shaped field. Shortly after this she married another silversmith, Benjamin Godfrey—their business was at the Sign of the Hand, Ring and Crown in Norris Street—but in 1741 he died, and she once more registered her own mark at the Goldsmiths' Hall and continued in business for seventeen years. During this time her products included soup tureens, cake baskets, salvers, and tea caddies.

Toward the south end of Haymarket you will find two imposing theaters nearly facing one another. On the right-hand side is Her Majesty's Theatre; it can be easily identified by the large green dome that caps the structure. The present French Renaissance–style theater, built in 1897, is the third on the site. The first, called The Queen's Theatre, opened in 1705 with *The Gamester*, an enormously popular comedy which had already had a good run at Lincoln's Inn Fields. The playwright was **Susannah Centlivre*** (d. 1723), a prolific and successful author. There is a story about Centlivre's youth which claims that she ran away from home when she was not yet sixteen and met a Cambridge student named Anthony Hammond on the road, who induced her to put herself under his protection. She disguised herself as a boy, according to the story, and lived with him in Cambridge for some time, studying grammar, logic, rhetoric, and ethics, and learning to fence. Eventually she moved on to London, where a more glorious fate awaited her.

Centlivre was not the only early eighteenth-century woman playwright whose plays were produced here. The Queen's Theatre also staged productions of plays by **Catherine Trotter*** (1679–1749), **Mary Delariviere Manley*** (1663–1724), and **Mary Pix*** (1666–before 1709).

A more recent event at Her Majesty's Theatre was the London debut of **Jenny Lind*** (1820–1887), the brilliant soprano known as "The Swedish Nightingale." Lind had been dreading her first trip to London, because she had unwisely signed a contract to sing at Drury Lane which she had never honored, and the management of that theater threatened her with prison if she set foot on British soil. However, Benjamin Lumley, of Her Majesty's, at last coaxed her into a season's work. She appeared for the first time in London on May 4, 1847, in the opera *Roberto il Diavolo*. Crowds surged through the theater doors when they opened at 7:30 P.M. Some theater-goers were carried off their feet by the mob; others had their dresses torn or their hats ruined. Queen Victoria and the Prince Consort were there to see the performance, and the queen sent a large arrangement of flowers to the stage when Lind took her bows.

Soon Jenny Lind was writing to her dear friend, Amalia Wichmann, "I am enchanted with England. . . . The English public has been unexampled in its kindness to me. . . . I leave my beloved England next Thursday. . . . " The management at Drury Lane stopped short of incarceration, but they did instigate a lawsuit, which they later won. Her Majesty's paid the damages.

Two years later, on May 10, 1849, Lind gave her final operatic appearance, again at Her Majesty's and in the same role. In spite of her great histrionic abilities, Lind never enjoyed opera, which she found too demanding. After she retired from the stage she confined herself to concert singing and oratorios. Her fondness for Britain continued: In 1858 she returned with her husband and family and made England her permanent home.

Across the street is the Theatre Royal, Haymarket, whose massive columns and classic portico were built by Nash in 1821. A theater has been on the site since 1720, when "the little Theatre in the Hay," as it was called to distinguish it from its larger rival across the street, opened without a charter or a patent. This situation had been remedied by the time **Helen Selina Sheridan's** comedy *Finesse* played there in 1863. Sheridan (1807–1867) was from a literary family. Her grandfather was the eighteenth-century playwright Richard Brinsley Sheridan—whose mother, Frances Sheridan*, was also a playwright. Helen's sister, **Caroline Norton** (1808–1877), was another writer. Norton, having lost a legacy, her own literary earnings, and custody of her three children to her husband, wrote in favor of the Divorce Bill and the first Married Women's Property Bill, writing bitterly: "I do not ask for my rights. I have no rights. I have only wrongs." The first Married Women's Property Act was passed by Parliament in 1857, in part because of Norton's much-publicized situation. Sheridan herself wrote poetry as well as plays, some of which was collected and published by her son in 1894, under the title *Poems and Verses*.

In December of 1881, **Lily Langtry*** (1853–1929) played Kate Hardcastle in *She Stoops to Conquer* at the Haymarket, and practically all London came to watch. Lily was already famous by the time of this, her London stage debut; her face was on penny-postcards all over town, and she had many devoted admirers. Oscar Wilde said of her: "I would rather have discovered Mrs. Langtry than to have discovered America. She is the most beautiful woman in the world." Her affairs were the talk of the town.

A strong-willed clergyman's daughter from the island of Jersey, she neglected her husband in favor of liaisons with more exciting men, the most prominent among them the Prince of Wales (later Edward VII). Lily was doubtful about an acting career. It seemed to her that to take up that not-quite-respectable profession might mean a loss in social status, when what she wanted above all was to be admitted to London's high society. She was also daunted by the prospect of such hard work. But in the end she couldn't refuse the promised salary or resist the challenge.

The critics were hard on Lily for some years, always assuming that her beauty and notoriety won more applause than her acting. But although she never became a great actress, in time she became a good one. She organized her own company and ran it very shrewdly, and she was especially noted for her enchanting portrayal of Rosalind in *As You Like It*. In later life she said of herself: "In life I have had all that I really wanted very much—a yacht, a racing stable, a theater of my own, lovely gardens." Some people are easy to please.

Retrace your steps toward Piccadilly Circus and turn right (east) into *Coventry Street*. En route to Leicester Square you will pass on your right-hand side the Prince of Wales Theatre, built in 1884. It was there, in 1896, that **Esme Beringer** (1875–1936) created a sensation by playing Romeo to her sister **Vera's** (1879–1964) Juliet. Esme was twenty-one, Vera only seventeen. Later on, the sisters wrote plays as well, having one play apiece produced on the stage in the 1933-34 season. Talent was a family tradition among the Beringers: Their mother, Aimee (nee Daniell), was a well-known playwright and novelist, and their father, Oscar, was a composer.

Coventry Street will deliver you to the northwest corner of *Leicester Square,* a large green surrounded by modern buildings and cinemas. The square is crowded with tourists: Any afternoon you can find a long line of them waiting at the booth that sells half-price theater tickets. In the late 1790s, however, the square was still residential, and **Elizabeth Inchbald*** (1753–1821), actress and playwright, lived on its east side. At this time in her life she was a widow. She had retired from acting, and was making quite a successful living by writing farces and comedies.

She lived alone, and very simply, doing her own housework. "I am both able and willing to perform bodily hard labor," she wrote to a friend in 1800. "But then the fatigue of being a fine lady the remaining part of the day is too much for any common strength."

Leave Leicester Square by Irving Street, at its southeast corner, and follow the curve of Charing Cross Road around until you reach *St. Martin's Lane*, another theatrical street. Here at its south end you will find the ornately decorated Coliseum, now the home of the English National Opera Company. It was built as a music hall in 1904, and its stage has seen performances by **Sarah Bernhardt*** (1844–1923), **Lily Langtry***, and **Ellen Terry*** (1847–1928).

Terry, one of the greatest actresses of her day, was born into a family of roving players. She joined the Haymarket Company in 1861, but left in 1864 to marry, returning to the stage after an absence of ten years. Audiences found her as captivating as ever. In 1878 she became leading lady to Henry Irving at the Lyceum (now gone), and they played opposite each other for twenty-five years, often in brilliant productions of Shakespeare. Her correspondence with George Bernard Shaw, which continued for many years before they finally met, was published in 1931. Terry was a member of the Actresses' Franchise League, an organization which performed one-act feminist plays throughout England in order to generate support for women's suffrage.

Travel north several blocks on St. Martin's Lane—you'll pass Cranbourne Street—then turn left (west) on West Street to reach *Cambridge Circus*. The circus is dominated by the Palace, the site of **Anna Pavlova's*** London debut in 1910. Pavlova (1882–1931) was already a famous ballerina with the (Russian) Imperial Ballet at this time. Though she had been a sickly child from a poor St. Petersburg family, she determined upon viewing *Sleeping Beauty* that she would become a ballet dancer, and in 1903 she first danced the role of Giselle, which she immortalized later in her career. In 1912 she bought a home in Hampstead, which she used as a base for the remainder of her life. The following year she formed her own ballet company, and for eighteen years she made one international tour after another. Her brilliant technique and charismatic appeal assured her of vast and devoted audiences wherever she went. In 1930 she danced the role of Giselle for the last time in the United Kingdom. The following year, about to embark upon yet another tour, she died suddenly of pneumonia. She was forty-nine years old.

Cross the circus on Shaftesbury Avenue, heading southwest toward *Wardour Street*, and when you reach it turn right (north) into the heart of Soho. On the right-hand side of the street as you head toward Old Compton Street is the tower of St. Anne's. Set back and above the street (the gardens were raised six feet above the pavement to make room for the more than ten thousand parishioners who are buried here), the green grass and tall, cool tower seem very English amid the cosmopolitan streets of Soho. At the base of the tower are buried the ashes of **Dorothy Sayers*** (1893–1957), writer, scholar, and translator, who was church warden here for some years. Besides translating Dante and writing essays on Anglican Christianity, Sayers created the delightful fictional detective, Lord Peter Wimsey, and his distinctly feminist companion Harriet Vane. Sayers' book *Gaudy Night*, in addition to being a mystery novel, is a query into whether marriage is possible for an independent woman.

The tower is all that remains of St. Anne's—the rest of the church was never rebuilt after bombing damage during the war—but in the original church, in 1763, Hester Salusbury became **Hester Thrale*** (1741–1821) by marrying, much against her will, the owner of a Southwark brewery. Mrs. Thrale later became acquainted with the Bluestockings, including Fanny Burney* and Mary Delany*, and, of course, with Dr. Johnson, in whose writings she is oftened mentioned.

Turn right into Old Compton Street, which over the years has been home to some of Soho's most noted restaurants, wine shops, and delicatessens, then left into *Frith Street*, and head north toward Soho Square. Here **Elizabeth Inchbald*** (1753–1821) lived in second-story lodgings while she was completing her novel, *A Simple Story*, in 1791. The hero of the book, a solemn, handsome young Catholic, is believed by many to be based upon Inchbald's friend, the actor John Kemble, brother to Sarah Siddons*. Inchbald (nee Simpson) was a farmer's daughter who married an actor, probably to get away from home. She was, like the heroine of *A Simple Story*, beautiful, lively, and assertive. (For example, she forced her husband to turn over to her the full amount of her salary, though he was under no legal obligation to do so.) When Elizabeth's husband died, there was a general expectation among their friends that she and Kemble would marry, but Kemble probably didn't offer himself, and perhaps it was just as well. A contemporary remarked that Kemble could never have endured a woman of such "independent temper."

In the same year, in *Dean Street*, just one street to the west, lived **Hester Chapone*** (1727–1801), another woman noted for her spirited and impulsive character. She was a member of the "Bluestocking" group—a derisive term applied to an intellectual society of women who preferred the writing of essays and discussion of literature to the pastimes of gossip and cards. Chapone was an intimate friend of Elizabeth Carter*, and addressed several odes to her. In addition to writing poetry, Chapone was a regular contributor to *Gentleman's Magazine*, but her most well-known work was *Letters on the Improvement of the Mind* (1774), a dissertation on the education of women in the form of letters originally written to a niece.

If you continue north on Frith Street it will take you into *Soho Square*, which was originally laid out in the 1680s. The square is mostly built up, but the Roman Catholic church of St. Patrick's, on the east side of the square, stands on the site of Carlisle House, which was acquired in the mid-eighteenth century by a Viennese opera singer named **Theresa Cornelys** (1723–1797). Cornelys, who became known as the Circe of Soho, was never quite respectable—one of her children was fathered by Casanova. But the assembly rooms she had erected in 1761, where dancing, cards, and concerts were provided for those who could pay the price, had many reputable patrons. The rooms were praised by Smollett in his novel *Humphrey Clinker*, and by Fanny Burney* in her journal. However, competition from a rival center caused Cornelys to lose her most influential clients, and she eventually went bankrupt. She died in Fleet Prison in 1797. The assembly rooms are still used by St. Patrick's today as part of the parish offices.

The designation "Fitzrovia" for the area north of Soho Square and west of Tottenham Court Road is an arguable one: Some people consider it a part of Marylebone South, others call it North Soho, bits of it could be considered part of Bloomsbury. From the north side of Soho Square take Soho Street across Oxford Street. Continue north on Rathbone Place until you cross Percy Street, then jog right into *Charlotte Street*. Several blocks to the north, just past the intersection of Charlotte and Goodge streets, is the site where the Scala Theatre once stood. Today the only sign of it is in the name of Scala Street, which comes in on your right. The theater was built in 1905 on a site which had been used for theater since 1772. On November 10, 1909, the theater presented a *Pageant of Great Women*, written by **Cicely Hamilton** and performed by members of the Actresses' Franchise League and other suffragettes. In addition to historic rulers such as Elizabeth I* and Catherine the Great, the suffragettes depicted some of Britain's military women, including Hannah Snell* and Mary Ann Talbot*.

In 1934, a play called *At What Price* was presented at the Scala for three nights, as a fund-raiser for The League of Coloured Peoples. The play was written by **Una Marson,** a Jamaican poet who was the publicity secretary for the league and editor of its magazine, *The Keys*. It was the first time a play written and performed by black people had been staged in Britain.

Turn right on Tottingham Street and left on *Whitfield Street*, and continue north for several blocks. As you head toward Grafton Way you will pass on your left the Montagu Centre, which bears a stone in its brick wall noting that the Hon. **Lilian Montagu*** (1873–1963) laid the foundation stone of the West Central Liberal Jewish Synagogue on May 20, 1951. Montagu was a social worker and a magistrate, a lay minister, and a prolific writer on liberal Judaism.

Continuing on toward Grafton Way, you will find at No. 108 Whitfield Street the **Marie Stopes*** House. Stopes (1880–1958) founded the first birth control clinic in London in 1921, and in 1925 it was moved to this site. Originally a botanist—she was an expert on fossil plants and in 1904 became the first woman on the science faculty of Manchester University—she turned her attention to the problem of contraception as a result of her first, unsatisfying marriage. Her approach differed from others who campaigned for birth control in that she advocated contraception as an aid to women's sexual pleasure, rather than as an attack upon poverty. She and her second husband fought many legal battles in their determination to provide contraception to women who wanted it. The Marie Stopes House is still a birth control and women's health clinic.

Turning left (west) on Grafton Way will take you into *Fitzroy Square*. The lovely, circular gardens are not open to the public,

Margaret Grace Bondfield

though there are some benches on the outside of the fence for those who want to rest their feet while looking through the railings. In 1894 the square witnessed a small but crucial incident in the history of women in the trade union movement. **Margaret Bondfield*** (1873–1953), a young West End shop assistant, was strolling through the square eating her fish and chips. When she was done, she perused the newspaper in which they had been wrapped and read there a letter from the secretary of the new National Union of Shop Assistants, Warehousemen, and Clerks. She joined up at once and rapidly became an important activist in the trade union movement. In 1899 she was the first woman delegate to a trade union conference. She worked with the Women's Trade Union League, was a member of the Independent Labour Party, helped to found the National Federation of Women Workers, and later worked with the Women's Cooperative Guild. In 1923 she became an M.P. for the Labour Party, representing Northampton, and in 1929 she became the first woman cabinet minister when she was appointed Minister of Labour.

On the north side of the square, which is now occupied largely by agencies and institutions, in the westernmost house, No. 19, **Louise Michel** (1830–1895) ran an "International Anarchist School" for children in the 1890s. A French anarchist and revolutionary, Michel fought on the barricades during the Paris Commune and was imprisoned several times for her radical activity. In 1890, after the French government refused to try her for her part in inciting workers in Vienna, she began a voluntary exile, joining revolutionaries from Russia, Germany, and elsewhere who formed a community in London. Michel liked London. "Yes, I admit it, I love this England, where my banished friends are always welcome," she wrote once. Michel's school came to an end when the police raided the building and discovered some bombs in the basement. Michel, however, was exonerated of any crime.

As you pass the southwest corner of the square, glance through the railings at a 1977 abstract sculpture by **Naomi Blake,** entitled *View.*

The plaque marking the house in which **Virginia Woolf***

(1882–1941) lived is at No. 29. She and her brother Adrian moved here from Gordon Square in March of 1907, at the time of her sister Vanessa's marriage. Some of her friends protested against the plan, considering the neighborhood disreputable, but Woolf, after checking with the police, disregarded their cautions. She lived here until 1911. She was at this time Virginia Stephen, and her first novel, *The Voyage Out*, would not be published until 1915, but she was already part of a star-studded literary and artistic circle called "the Bloomsbury group."

To reach the Warren Street tube station, retrace your steps along Grafton Way and continue east to Tottenham Court Road, then turn left.

9
Westminster

Begin: Tate Gallery (Nearest Tube Station: Pimlico)
End: St. James's Park Tube Station

Westminster is the seat of government, and the seat of government is always the scene of protest. Thus it is that the streets of Westminster are haunted by the strident cries of the suffragettes, who repeatedly flooded Whitehall, Downing Street, Parliament Square, and the Houses of Parliament in their indefatigable labors to win the vote for women.

But before you follow in the footsteps of the suffragettes, you would do well to have a look around the Tate Gallery†, easily reached by busses 88 and 77A, or from the nearby Pimlico tube station. The Tate specializes in works by British artists and in twentieth century painting and sculpture, so women are somewhat better represented here than at the National Gallery. However, the collections do rotate, so if you want to be sure of seeing a particular work, it's best to make an appointment. (Try to notify the museum about a week in advance.)

The Tate houses several sculptures by **Barbara Hepworth***
(1903–1975). Hepworth and her first husband, the sculptor John

Skeaping, both belonged to a radical artists' group called the Seven and Five Society in the thirties. Her early, stylized work soon became abstract, and though her personal life contained many disappointments, her achievements as an abstract sculptor have assured her of an important place in art history. She died in a fire at her studio in St. Ives.

Several paintings by **Gwen John*** (1876–1939) belong to the Tate Gallery. Sister to the painter Augustus John, she followed him to the Slade School, and later studied in Paris. After 1903 she lived permanently in France. She was a model for and lover of Rodin, and a friend of Rilke. John was interested in mysticism and joined the Roman Catholic Church in 1913. Her passionate love for her friend Vera Oumancoff evidently disturbed that woman. Vera wrote to Gwen that she thought the attachment was bad for Gwen's soul. "I am well aware that you have great sensitivity," she chided, "but you must direct it to Our Lord, towards the Blessed Virgin."

Another woman painter represented in the Tate is **Vanessa Bell*** (1879–1961). Bell came from the talented Stephen family— she was Virginia Woolf's* older sister. It was she who founded the discussion group known as the Friday Club in 1905, where those bright intellectuals who were later known as the Bloomsbury Group first began to come together. She married the art historian Clive Bell in 1907, but the marriage was not successful, and she spent a number of years living with the painter Duncan Grant.

In 1912 Bell exhibited four paintings at Roger Fry's second Post-Impressionist Exhibition, which featured the works of such painters as Braque, Picasso, Matisse, and Cezanne. She was one of the first British abstract painters (though she returned to representational work in later years) and was a member of the London Group. She also did decorative art, designing textiles and ceramics, as well as book covers for Woolf's Hogarth Press.

Just south of the Tate Gallery you will find the Royal Army Medical Corps, a big brick building guarded by an iron fence. The RAMC is not open to the public, but its school features a room named for one of the most interesting female physicians in Britain's history: Dr. **James Barry** (1795?–1865).

Barry, who was born Miranda Stuart, is said to have disguised herself as a boy in order to study medicine at the University of Edinburgh. Still passing as a man, she became an army surgeon and practiced her profession around the world, living many years in Cape Town. Many things are claimed about James Barry. It is said that she was cantankerous, hard to work with, and easily offended. She is credited by some with having performed the second completely successful cesarean section in the western world. She was merciless to "quack" doctors and apothecaries, and was a constant reformer, demanding humane treatment for lepers and an improvement in conditions of prisons where she treated convicts. Her private life, though shrouded with secrecy, generated many rumors: It was said that she was a vegetarian and a teetotaler; that she was flirtatious with women; that she was once accused of engaging in sodomy with a man.

But the most dramatic story in the life of James Barry is the one that occurred after her death, when she was laid out by Sally Bishop, who was amazed to discover that the corpse was a woman. Dr. James Barry is buried in Kensal Green Cemetery, London.

A more recent practitioner of military medicine was **Christine Moody.** Her father, Harold Moody, was a Jamaican doctor practicing in London and the first president of the League of Coloured Peoples. Christine received her medical degree during World War II, and after a brief period of private practice joined the Royal Army Medical Corps, where she became a captain and served in India.

Head north on Millbank, passing the Tate Gallery on your left, and follow it along the Thames about a half mile, until you reach the *Victoria Tower Gardens*, a shady triangle of green next to the Houses of Parliament. In the heart of the garden stands a cast of *The Burghers of Calais*, by Auguste Rodin. In the year 1346, when the French seaport of Calais had lain under siege for a year, the town's elders came out to surrender to the English king Edward III. They appeared wearing halters around their necks, offering to forfeit their lives in the hope that their city would be saved from the sacking and devastation of war. Thanks to the intervention of **Philippa of Hainault*** (1314–1369), Edward's queen, not

Emmeline Pankhurst

only the city but the lives of the burghers themselves were spared. The sculpture was commissioned by the town of Calais, but once it was finished there was much controversy about whether it should be erected, possibly because the authorities wanted the burghers to look uniformly noble, whereas the six figures in Rodin's life-sized group show varying states of mind from despair to defiance.

In the northwest corner of the gardens, facing Abingdon

Street, you will find a bronze statue of **Emmeline Pankhurst***
(1858–1928), erected in 1930. A low, curved wall extends in either
direction from the base of the statue, ending in a plinth at each
end, and on one of these is a medallion to **Christabel Pankhurst***
(1880–1958), Emmeline's daughter. These two were the charismatic if despotic leaders of the Women's Social and Political
Union, founded by Emmeline in 1903. Mrs. Pankhurst devoted
most of her life to working for women's suffrage, and by the time
she died while campaigning for Parliament in 1928 she had
become a national hero. Christabel also stood for Parliament in
1918, but was defeated. Later on she became an evangelical
Christian and preached the second coming through her best-
selling tracts.

On the left side of the plinth is a bronze replica of the WSPU
prisoner's badge. Between 1905 and 1914, over a thousand women earned the right to wear this emblem. Emmeline Pankhurst
herself was imprisoned and released thirteen times during the
years 1912–13, under what was popularly known as the "Cat and
Mouse" act. Passed in order to avoid forced feedings, the act
mandated the release of prisoners who engaged in hunger
strikes once their health began to deteriorate. But the women
were rearrested the moment they again showed themselves in
public or tried to participate in militant activity, on the ground
that they were once more fit to serve their prison sentences.
Emmeline Pankhurst's health was severely injured during these
years, and it was probably only the coming of World War I and
the WSPU's decision to cease militant activity for its duration
that saved her from martyrdom to the cause.

One can't help reflecting that the WSPU prisoner's emblem
occupies a spot which could easily have held a memorial to
Sylvia Pankhurst* (1882–1960), who designed the badge in
question. She herself was imprisoned many times and was forcibly fed while on a hunger strike. But her break with the WSPU
at the outbreak of World War I, her radicalism, advocacy of "free
love," and her concern for the Ethiopian struggles that were
taking place in the thirties, perhaps made her a less estimable
figure in the eyes of the authorities.

Proceed north on Abingdon Street as it becomes *St. Margaret*

Street, and you will find yourself passing between two of the greatest tourist attractions in London. Westminster Abbey (see next chapter) will be on your left, and the Houses of Parliament on your right. The administrative center of the kingdom has been here at Westminster Palace since the time of Edward the Confessor, and the House of Commons has met on this site since the Reformation. The present Gothic-style buildings were constructed in the mid-nineteenth century to the designs of Charles Barry and Augustus Pugin, though they were extensively rebuilt after severe bombing damage during World War II.

The militant suffragettes made many demonstrations on this site, but theirs were not the first efforts at female enfranchisement. On June 7, 1866, **Emily Davies*** (1830–1921) and **Elizabeth Garrett Anderson*** (then Garrett) (1836–1917) arrived at Westminster Hall carrying the first petition demanding women's suffrage. They had arranged with John Stuart Mill that they should present it to him, but when they arrived he was nowhere in sight, and the women were somewhat taken aback by the stares of the many men who stood about chatting. They carried the petition roll—which bore fifteen hundred signatures—over to the only other woman in sight, an apple seller. The vendor obligingly hid the petition under her stall, but upon finding out what it was insisted upon signing it before returning it to Davies and Garrett. The document was at last presented to Mill, who presented it in turn to Parliament. But fifty-two years elapsed before women secured the vote.

When they were finally enfranchised, of course, women also won the right to seek office, and they lost no time taking advantage of the opportunity. **Nancy Astor*** (1879–1964) is usually considered the first woman M.P., but she was not the first to be elected. In 1918, the first year women were permitted to run for office, Countess **Constance Markiewicz** (1868–1927) was the only woman who won a seat when she was elected M.P. from Dublin. Markiewicz's path led her from society beauty to trade unionist and Sinn Feiner, and she married a Polish painter along the way. She was condemned to death for her part in the Easter Rising which took place in Dublin in 1916, but the sentence was later changed to life imprisonment, and with other rebels she was given amnesty in 1917. However, at the time of her election she had not yet been released from prison. Together with the other Republican M.P.s she refused to sit in "an alien Parliament." So it was that Nancy Astor, elected in 1919 to replace her husband (who had moved to the House of Lords upon the death of his father), became the first woman to take her seat in the Parliament of Great Britain.

Other women followed. In 1924 **Ellen Wilkinson** (1891–1947) became a Labour Party M.P. Daughter of a Lancashire cotton worker, she was known as "Red Ellen," partly because of her hair and partly because of her politics. She was active in both the suffrage and the labor movements, and was a member of Britain's Communist Party from 1920 to 1924. In 1923 **Margaret Bondfield*** (1873–1953), later the first woman cabinet minister, was first elected to Parliament. She was Minister of Labour from 1929 to 1931, when she lost her seat to Conservative M.P. **Irene Ward** as part of the general collapse of the Labour government. Ward campaigned for the shipbuilding and fishing industries, and also for legislation that improved conditions for nurses and midwives. She was known for her back-bench heckling and her outspoken ways, and was once suspended from the House of Commons for five days for calling the Labour Government a dictatorship. **Jennie Lee** (1904–1988), daughter of a Scottish miner, became an M.P. for the Independent Labour Party in 1929, when she was twenty-four years old. She was active in the socialist and labor movements and served in the House until she retired in 1970.

Edith and **Shirley Summerskill** were something a little different in the political arena: a mother and daughter legislative team. Edith (1901–1980), a doctor who married a doctor, was first elected in 1938. As a Labour M.P. she campaigned for national health insurance, preventive medicine, and women's rights, not shying away from controversial subjects like prostitution and cohabitation. In 1959, as Under Secretary at the Ministry of Food, she was responsible for the Clean Milk Act. She also campaigned against boxing and smoking. Her daughter Shirley (b. 1931) took her mother's name instead of her father's, and became, like her mother, first an M.D. and then an M.P. She was elected to the House of Commons in 1964.

More recent women M.P.s have included **Barbara Ann Castle** (b. 1911), Fabian, socialist, and journalist, who was first elected in 1945 and who carried the Equal Pay Act through Parliament in 1970 (the act became effective in 1975). In 1959 **Judith Hart*** (b. 1924) became Labour M.P. for Lanark, but her greatest impact was as Minister of Overseas Development, in which capacity she spoke and wrote about the United Kingdom's moral responsibilities to Third World countries.

As you continue north on St. Margaret Street, you will pass *Parliament Square* on your left. Suffragettes often gathered at the square, sometimes marching there from Caxton Hall or Albert Hall. On other occasions, such as June 30, 1908, the leadership of the WSPU issued a call to the public to gather there. On that particular evening, a crowd estimated to be a hundred thousand strong mobbed the square. Many had come to jeer or to watch the fun, others to support. "From the steps of public buildings, from stone copings, from the iron railings of the Palace Yard, to which they clung precariously, our women made speeches until the police pulled them down and flung them into the moving, swaying, excited crowds," Emmeline Pankhurst wrote. Again and again the women tried to reach the House of Commons but were repelled by mounted policemen. The battle lasted from eight until midnight, and many Members of Parliament, including Lloyd George, Herbert Gladstone, and Winston Churchill (whose statue is now in the square) came out to watch.

As you turn right onto Bridge Street you will see a monument to a far more ancient protest than that of the suffragettes. At the west end of *Westminster Bridge,* on its north side, is an awe-inspiring statue of **Boudica** (also spelled Boudicca and Boadicea), Britain's great warrior queen. When her husband died without a male heir, his will specified that half of his estate should go to his family and half to the Emperor Nero. In this way he hoped to appease the Roman authorities in Britain and protect his family. But the Romans disregarded his will and fell upon the estate, flogging Boudica, raping her daughters, and annexing her lands. Boudica rallied her tribe, the Iceni, and led an army on a rampage through the Roman towns, sacking the cities now known as Colchester, St. Alban's, and London, and massacring seventy thousand Romans in the process. In A.D. 62 she was at last decisively defeated and is said to have taken poison rather than submit to capture. The statue depicts the queen of the Iceni in her war chariot, horses plunging before her, while her daughters, one on either side, look on in dismay.

As you cross the bridge, you will be heading due east, just as **Dorothy Wordsworth** (1771–1855) did at dawn the morning of July 31, 1802, as she and her brother William set off on a trip to the Continent. William's *Sonnet Composed Upon Westminster Bridge* is well-known, but Dorothy's record of the same moment is in prose.

> *It was a beautiful morning. The city, St. Paul's, with the river and a multitude of little boats, made a most beautiful sight as we crossed Westminster Bridge. The houses were not overhung by their cloud of smoke, and they were spread out endlessly, yet the sun shone so brightly, with such a fierce light, that there was even something like the purity of one of nature's own grand spectacles.*

Dorothy's journals, published thirty years after her death, record her impressions of life and nature. Her descriptions seem also to have frequently provided points of departure for the poetry her brother hammered out in their cottage in the Lake District.

Rather confusingly, heading due east brings you to the South Bank of the Thames, where you'll find the South Bank Lion. This immense, fuzzy-looking beast once stood outside the Lambeth factory of **Eleanor Coade*** (d. 1796). The lion is made of Coade Stone, an artificial stone which was the most weatherproof that had ever been made, manufactured between the 1760s and 1840. It was originally invented by Richard Holt in the 1720s, but was improved and chiefly manufactured under the supervision of Eleanor Coade and her daughter, also named Eleanor. The secret of making Coade Stone has since been lost. The lion itself was made in 1837.

Walk back to the west side of the river, enjoying the famous view of the Houses of Parliament and Big Ben, properly called the Clock Tower (Big Ben is the name of the bell). As you glance at the buildings that line the *Victoria Embankment*, to your right, you will see the Cannon Row Police Station. On the morning of February 14, 1907, fifty-seven women and two men were arraigned there, two and three at a time. Their crime, of attempting to carry to Parliament a resolution in favor of women's suffrage, had occurred the day before and had been broken up by mounted police. **Christabel Pankhurst*** was the first to stand before the magistrate. Upon being told that the "disgraceful scenes" of the suffragettes must cease, she replied: "The scenes can be stopped in only one way." The magistrate offered her a choice, twenty shillings or fourteen days. Christabel chose prison, of course, as did all the suffragettes tried that day. **Charlotte Despard*** (1844–1939) and **Sylvia Pankhurst*** were given three weeks each.

According to Emmeline Pankhurst, in the first few months of 1907 "the English Government sent to prison one hundred and thirty women whose 'militancy' consisted merely of trying to carry a resolution from a hall to the Prime Minister in the House of Commons."

When you have reached Parliament Square once more, turn right into *Parliament Street*, which becomes Whitehall as you follow it north. In December of 1911 **Emily Wilding Davison** (1872–1913) attempted to burn a letter box in Parliament Street, for which act she received a six-month prison sentence. Her deed was called "prophetic" by Emmeline Pankhurst in later years, as it foreshadowed the policy of arson in the militant suffragist movement. Davison was among the most fanatic of the suffragettes. During one of her many imprisonments she threw herself down a flight of stairs to protest the treatment of her sister prisoners, and in 1913, on Derby Day, without orders but wearing the suffragette colors, she ran onto the racecourse to try to seize the reins of the king's horse. She was badly injured in the resulting accident and died a few hours later.

The entrance to *Downing Street*, blocked and guarded, will be on your left as you head north on Whitehall. As the residence of the Prime Minister, No. 10 Downing Street was the target of much suffragette activity. On January 17, 1908, **Edith New*** and Nurse **Olivia Smith** chained themselves to the railings in front of the house, to prevent themselves from being taken quickly away, to prolong their protest, and also to express the "political bondage of womanhood," in the words of Sylvia Pankhurst. While the police were struggling with the chains, **Flora Drummond*** (1869–1940) dashed up to the house and managed to enter, almost reaching the Council Chambers before she was seized and thrown bodily out of the building. She was then arrested, of course.

Six months later, No. 10 Downing Street became the site of the first window-breaking in suffragette history, when the unquenchable **Edith New*** and **Mary Leigh** threw stones through the windows of what was then Herbert Henry Asquith's official residence. They notified Emmeline Pankhurst from police court that, since they had acted without orders, they would understand if they were repudiated by headquarters. "Far from repudiating them," Mrs. Pankhurst later wrote, "I went at once to see them in their cells, and assured them of my approval of their act. The smashing of windows is a time-honored method of showing displeasure in a political situation."

A mass action at Downing Street occurred on November 18, 1910, when hundreds of women broke through the police cordon there in spite of being pushed and struck by the officers. The day became known as Black Friday because of the brutality of the police.

The end result of all this activity, of course, was that in 1918 women over thirty in Great Britain received the right to vote. (The Flapper Vote Act of 1928 extended the franchise to women twenty-one and over.) Sixty-one years after that, **Margaret Thatcher*** (b. 1925) became the first woman Prime Minister of Great Britain. Sylvia Pankhurst would have been horrified; one is less certain about Emmeline and Christabel.

As you retrace your steps down *Whitehall,* you might recall the general day of militancy on November 21, 1911, when women wreaked havoc on the government offices up and down the street, damaging the Treasury, the Scottish Education Office, the War Office, and the National Liberal Club, among others. Miss **Billinghurst** was arrested in her wheelchair, which was carried shoulder-high by the four policemen who took her off to court.

Cross Bridge Street again and go around the south side of

Parliament Square, following the curve of the road as it leads past Westminster Abbey, and continue southwest on *Victoria Street*. Just past its intersection with Broadway you will come to a little square of green on the right-hand side of the street. Within this park is an unusual, scroll-shaped memorial to the activities of the suffragettes, erected by the Suffrage Fellowship. It's a fitting spot for a memorial, for if you take the pedestrian walk in the northwest corner of the square it will lead you to *Caxton Street*, where stands the ornate red brick building Caxton Hall, often used by the suffragettes for mass meetings. Emmeline Pankhurst dated the beginning of the militant movement to a meeting held in Caxton Hall on February 19, 1906. While **Annie Kenney*** (1879–1953) was engaged in speaking, Mrs. Pankhurst received word that no mention of women's suffrage had been made in the Liberal Government's program for the parliamentary session. She urged the women there to follow her to the House of Commons, and to demand of the M.P.s there that they introduce a women's suffrage bill. The assembly rushed to the House in a body, but were denied entrance to the Strangers' Gallery. They stood about in the cold rain and were finally allowed to enter twenty at a time. Women waited for hours for their turns, and no M.P. was persuaded to introduce the resolution they sought. But Emmeline Pankhurst wrote of that day:

> Out of the disappointment and dejection of that experience I yet reaped a richer harvest of happiness than I had ever known before. Those women had followed me to the House of Commons. They had defied the police. They were awake at last. They were prepared to do something that women had never done before— fight for themselves. Women had always fought for men, and for their children. Now they were ready to fight for their own human rights. Our militant movement was established.

To get to the St. James's Park tube station, head east on Caxton Street, then turn left (north) on Broadway.

10

Westminster Abbey

Begin and End: Westminster Tube Station

Westminster Abbey†, that ancient maze of aisles and niches, chapels and cloisters, is crowded with dead people, including large numbers of women. Here women have been crowned, married, honored, and above all, buried. It would be impossible or in any case dull to list every woman who molders within the Abbey precincts, but I have pointed the way toward the tombs and memorials of greatest interest to the feminist traveller. These remembered women may be royal or obscure, political, theatrical, or literary. Some of them were eccentric, though few went so far as to be poor.

Touring the Abbey, especially at the height of the tourist season, is a challenge. The crowds are dense and are guided with dispatch through a system of lines and barricades. It is easy to get stuck viewing something you had no intention of seeing or to get rushed past the one thing you came to see. Be stubborn and persevere, and if you get lost ask one of the Abbey employees or volunteers for assistance. They are astonishingly familiar with the cluttered aisles and chapels, and will be happy to direct you or even lead you to the monument you're seeking. Please note that there is a charge to view some parts of the Abbey. This gives added difficulty to crossing back and forth, and you'll have an easier time of it if you try not to fight the system more than you can help. No matter how long you wander among the tombstones, there is no danger that you will be locked in for the night as that eighteenth-century lady of letters, **Letitia Pilkington*** (1712–1750), once was. She spent the night in the pulpit, wrapped in a carpet from the communion table to protect herself from the rats.

A church may have been on or near this site as early as 604. It is certain that Edward the Confessor built a new church and monastic buildings in this location, and it was in that church, in 1154, that **Eleanor of Aquitaine** (1122–1204), one of England's most fascinating queens, was crowned in a ceremony of great grandeur and splendor. When married to her first husband, Louis VII of France, Eleanor organized a Queen's Guard of noblewomen and rode with Louis on a crusade. But the king couldn't abide her flirtatiousness, and their marriage was annulled—six weeks before she married Henry Plantagenet, later Henry II of England. She spent sixteen years imprisoned by him after encouraging their sons to rebel against him, but when her son, Richard the Lionheart, came to the throne in 1189, she became a person of great power and importance once more. She influenced matters of government greatly while Richard was away at the Crusades, and when he returned they attended state functions together. (Richard had married Berengaria of Navarre, but never brought his wife to England; he had little interest in family life and left no heirs.)

Nothing now remains of the church in which Eleanor of Aquitaine was crowned; the oldest parts of the present Abbey date back to 1245—a mere seven and a half centuries of history are impressed upon its stones. After you have been round the exterior of the Abbey to admire its ancient walls, enter by the west door, under the eighteenth-century towers of Portland stone.

The Nave

To your left as you enter you'll find a black diamond on the floor commemorating the philanthropist **Angela Burdett-Coutts*** (1814–1906), who died at age ninety-three after doing an almost incalculable amount of good. Her body lay in state in her home while thousands of the poor filed past to pay their final respects, and her funeral was attended by aristocracy and coster-mongers, statesmen and flower girls.

The floor slab to **Beatrice Webb*** (1858–1943), Fabian and socialist, and to her husband Sidney, is on the same side of the church, near the north wall (just before the imposing memorial to Charles Fox). Sidney and Beatrice married in 1892, and theirs was a highly successful partnership, as they were both prolific writers and dedicated activists. In 1929 Sidney was created first Baron Passfield, but Beatrice refused the designation of Lady Passfield.

On the opposite (south) side of the church, in St. George's Chapel (the glass-walled chapel designated for private prayer), is an oak screen commemorating the suffragist **Millicent Fawcett*** (1847–1929). The inscription notes that "she won citizenship for women" (though it should perhaps be mentioned that she did not accomplish this single-handedly). Fawcett's feminist instincts surfaced early; as a girl, while getting ready for a ball, she heard two older girls discussing a married woman of their acquaintance. "Look how he dresses her," one said, and Millicent fumed silently at the degradation and dependence implied.

Fawcett was a speaker on behalf of women's suffrage for fifty years, though she was never wholly comfortable in the role. In her memoirs she claims that when she first heard of the victory in 1918 her immediate thought was: "Then I shall never have to make another suffrage speech!"

Return to the Nave and begin to make your way down the South Aisle. You'll soon come to a small square bearing the name and death date of **Ann Oldfield*** (1683–1730), the actress. A jingle of the day commented on her death, "This we must own, in justice to her shade/'Tis the first bad exit OLDFIELD ever made." Bad it may have been, but it couldn't have been more lavish. According to her maid, she went to her grave in "a very fine Brussels lace head, a holland shift and double ruffles of the same lace, a pair of new kid gloves, and . . . a winding-sheet." In addition to being a fine actress, Oldfield bore two children, though she never married. Queen Caroline once commented to the actress on the rumor that she had married her lover, Charles Churchill. "So it is said, Your Royal Highness," Oldfield replied, "but we have not owned it yet." Brigadier General Churchill applied for permission to erect a monument to Oldfield's memory, but it was refused by the dean of the Abbey, so her latter-day admirers must be content with this modest plaque.

Further along the South Aisle (possibly on the other side of the barrier) you'll find a wall plaque elaborately framed with miniature marble columns. The gold letters record the burial of **Dorothy Osborne*** (1627–1695) and her husband Sir William Temple, to whom she wrote the letters that have given historians such a vivid picture of day-to-day life in the Commonwealth era. They corresponded for years before they were finally permitted to become engaged, and then, on the eve of their wedding, Dorothy contracted smallpox, a disease much feared by seventeenth-century beauties. Temple married her in spite of her pitted face, and they lived together for forty-one years before Dorothy died.

Crossing to the North Aisle, you'll find near the entrance to the North Choir Aisle a plaque to the astronomer William Herschel, but none to his sister **Caroline Herschel*** (1750–1848). German Jews who emigrated to England, the two often worked together, and Caroline discovered fourteen nebulae and eight comets on her own. Fanny Burney* wrote in her diary of Caroline's first discovery: "The comet was small and had nothing grand or striking in its appearance, but it is the first lady's comet and I was very desirous to see it." After her brother's death Caroline returned to Hanover.

You must now pay to enter the rest of the Abbey, a procedure which is likely to occur at the entrance to the North Choir Aisle.

North Choir Aisle and Transept

A glass-topped case housing the illustrated Roll of Honour of the Women's Voluntary Service, 1939–45, stands near the entrance to the North Choir Aisle. Here are recorded the names of the women who died during World War II in the performance of their duties. Formed in 1938, the WVS, which had chapters all through the nation as well as in London, was closely allied with Civil Defense. Its activities included much desperately needed "women's work," such as running mobile canteens and laundry units, making hospital supplies ranging from bandages to pajamas, mending troop uniforms, and establishing emergency clothes depots (over 150 in London, more than two thousand in England). In at least one county, women in the WVS were asked to teach soldiers how to darn socks. The WVS also conducted large-scale recycling campaigns to counter shortages of paper, aluminum, and tin; trained air-wardens; gave courses in air-raid procedures, including extinguishing incendiary bombs and fire fighting; and helped to administer government evacuation programs.

In the North Transept you will find a large canopied monument, almost hemmed in by the statues near it. The monument was built by William Cavendish, the Duke of Newcastle, in his lifetime, to commemorate himself and his second wife, **Margaret Cavendish,** Duchess of Newcastle (1624–1674). She and her husband were both scribblers, but Margaret in particular filled volume upon volume with plays, verses, biography, and her own reflections upon life, examining such questions as why dogs wag their tails when happy and whether small amounts of opium may benefit lunatics. Her writing and her eccentric style of dress (she designed the fashions for herself and her household) made her a ridiculous figure to many of her contemporaries. Dorothy Osborne* (whose monument is in the Nave) wrote of Margaret's poetry: "They say it is ten times more extravagant than her dress. Sure, the poor woman is a little distracted, she could never be so ridiculous else as to venture at writing books, and in verse, too." However, the duchess was much loved and admired by her duke, and some 250 years after her death Virginia Woolf* wrote of the Duchess of Newcastle, "There is something noble and Quixotic and high-spirited, as well as crack-brained and bird witted, about her." The recumbent effigy of the duchess holds an open book, a pen case, and an inkhorn, and more books are shown on the south side of the tomb.

King Henry VII's Chapel

At the far east end of Westminster Abbey is the magnificent Henry VII Chapel (stairs), built under the patronage of that king in the opening years of the sixteenth century. The chapel competes successfully with that of Edward the Confessor for Most Royalty Buried Within, though only a few of the regal corpses are mentioned here. As you head toward the stairs you may want to stop in at the Chapel of St. John the Baptist (two steps up). There, in a columned niche against the wall, is a memorial to Mrs. **Mary Kendall** (1677–1709), which depicts a sweet, prim-looking young woman. Her virtues are described in great detail on the monument, which mentions the "close Union and Friendship in which she liv'd with the Lady Catharine Jones, and in testimony of which she desir'd that even their Ashes after Death might not be divided." The title "Mrs." was once commonly used in England among married and unmarried women alike.

The nave of the Henry VII Chapel is dominated by the tomb of Henry himself, who lies with his wife, **Elizabeth of York** (1466–1503). Elizabeth was Yorkist heir to the throne after the murder of her brothers, a deed which some attribute to Richard III. Her marriage to the Lancastrian heir Henry Tudor ended the Wars of the Roses. Elizabeth, known for her gentleness, also wrote poetry, including the sestina "My Heart Is Set Upon a Lusty Pin."

The most interesting woman honored in Westminster Abbey is without a doubt St. **Wilgefortis,** also known as St. Uncumber. If you look above the archway over the tomb of Ludovic Stuart, you will see her statue—she's the bearded figure carrying a cross, on the far right of the statue-filled niche. According to the story, Wilgefortis was one of nine daughters of a Portuguese king. Betrothed against her will to the pagan king of Sicily, St.

Wilgefortis prayed that God would disfigure her so that she'd be unattractive to men. When a beard grew on her chin, her lover rejected her, and her irate father had her crucified. For centuries women encumbered with unwelcome husbands have made offerings of oats to the saint, giving rise to the jingle: If you cannot sleep or slumber/Give some oats to St. Uncumber.

In the North Aisle of the chapel is the white marble tomb of **Elizabeth I*** (1533–1603), one of the most brilliant and best-loved sovereigns of England. Her reign saw currency reform, the enactment of poor laws, and prosperity in agriculture and commerce. Under her, England became a top-ranking European power, defeated Spain, and began colonization.

Elizabeth had what it takes to be the ruler of such a nation. When the Spanish Armada was en route to England, the queen reviewed her troops at Tilbury, mounted on a horse and clad in a suit of armor. She offered "to lay down for my God, and for my Kingdom, and for my people, my honour and my blood, even in the dust. I know I have the body of a weak, feeble woman, but I have the heart and stomach of a king, and a king of England, too." However, her blood was not required, as the British Navy defeated the Armada, without the help of ground troops.

The indomitable queen never allowed her gender to inhibit her authority. Once she spoke sternly to one of her councillors in the frank idiom of her era, saying, "Had I been born crested, not cloven, you would not speak thus to me."

Elizabeth was a well-educated woman. Her studies included geography, math, and astronomy, and she attained early fluency in French, Italian, and Spanish. Her court was always a center of learning; the Elizabethan era was the era of Shakespeare, Spenser, and Bacon. Elizabeth herself wrote poetry, including a brief verse composed when she was imprisoned: "Written With a Diamond on Her Window at Woodstock."

Beneath the tomb of Elizabeth lies the coffin of her older half sister, **Mary I*** (1516–1558), the first woman to rule England in her own right. Raised by her mother, Catherine of Aragon*, to be an ardent Catholic, she renounced the church in order to be granted succession rights but continued to practice the banned Latin mass in secret. Her five-year reign was not a happy one:

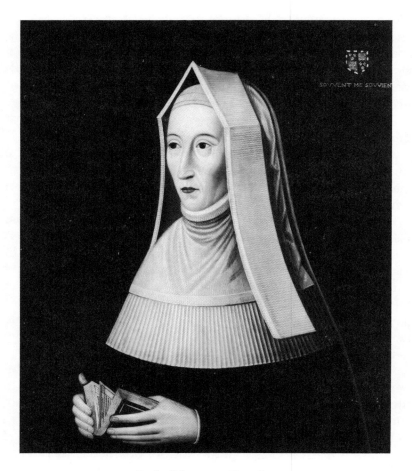

Lady Margaret Beaufort

Her desire to restore England to Catholicism led her to the burning of Protestant martyrs at Smithfield; her marriage to Philip of Spain was unpopular because of anti-Spanish sentiment, and she engaged in a war with France which resulted in the loss of Calais—the last English possession on the Continent. Her husband left her when Parliament refused to crown him, and she was left lonely, ill, and childless.

In the South Aisle of the chapel lie yet more queens, but none laid to rest so grandly as **Mary,** Queen of Scots* (1524–1587).

Mary became queen of Scotland when she was six days old, but didn't begin her reign until 1561. She spent most of her years on the throne trying to hang onto it, and at last failed, being forced to abdicate in favor of her son, later James VI of Scotland and James I of England—the first ruler of a united England and Scotland. After her abdication she fled to England, but her personal popularity and fervent Roman Catholicism made her a threat to Elizabeth I, and after she was involved in several plots aimed at gaining the English throne, Elizabeth reluctantly signed her death warrant.

Mary was fond of chess, billiards, and backgammon, as well as deerhunting, archery, golf, and pall mall. She was skilled at needlecraft and in the early days of her reign used to take a piece of sewing along to meetings of the Privy Council. She also did a lot of embroidery during her long imprisonment in England—in between hatching plots, one supposes.

In the same chamber as the Queen of Scots lies the tomb of Lady **Margaret Beaufort*** (1443–1509), for whom Lady Margaret Hall at Oxford is named. Elizabeth Wordsworth, founder of the college, chose the name because "she was a gentlewoman, a scholar and a saint, and after being married three times she took a vow of celibacy; what more could be expected of any woman?" The effigy is a beautiful and moving portrait of Margaret in her old age. Note especially the wrinkled hands raised in prayer.

At the east end of the South Aisle you will find the tombs of two more sovereign sisters. **Mary II*** (1662–1694) ruled jointly with her husband, William of Orange, after they deposed her father, James II, in the Glorious Revolution of 1688. Though Mary was the successor to the throne, she insisted upon being crowned jointly with William, who was her cousin, and in fact ruled only when he was away on campaigns.

Mary's younger sister **Anne*** (1665–1714), on the other hand, was sovereign in her own right for thirteen years. Though she was much influenced by her close advisers—including her favorite, Sarah Churchill* (the Duchess of Marlborough)—Anne was herself a lover of political intrigue, and in addition to a good helping of common sense, she possessed a stubborn desire to rule England well. In spite of poor health, she put enormous amounts of time and energy into studying affairs of state, and showed a determination not to be bullied on account on her sex. On one occasion she told one of her ministers: "Whoever of ye Whigs thinks I am to be Heckter'd or frighted into a Complyance tho I am a woman, are mightey mistaken in me."

Chapel of Saint Edward the Confessor

When you enter the Confessor's Chapel (stairs) you are approaching royalty in a serious way: In addition to the saint himself, at least five kings and five queens (not all in matched sets) lie nearby. **Catherine de Valois** (1401–1437), queen of Henry V, shares her husband's tomb at the east end of the Confessor's Chapel. For over two hundred years her embalmed body lay in an open coffin, and in 1669 Pepys wrote in his diary that he had kissed the dead queen on the mouth. **Edith** (1020?–1075), queen of Edward the Confessor, is said to be buried near his shrine. Edith was well educated in the nunnery at Wilton and married Edward in 1045. After five years it became clear that the marriage was barren, and the king sent Edith into the keeping of her sister, the Abbess of Wherwell, while he sought a divorce. For two years Edith's family and Edward engaged in a political struggle in which the question of divorce was but one element. But in 1052, Edith returned to her role as queen, and though she never gave Edward an heir, she became an influential counselor, especially in the matter of ecclesiastical appointments.

Queen **Maud** (1080–1118), first queen of Henry I, lies buried in an unknown location somewhere in the Abbey, but her resting place may be near this spot. Also known as Matilda of Scotland, Maud was placed at a young age in the care of an aunt who was an abbess. The aunt was quite determined that Maud should become a nun; Maud was equally determined that she should not. There is a story that the aunt went so far as to put the veil on Maud's hair, but that as soon as she turned her back Maud took it off and stamped on it. However, she is said to have worn it willingly when visited by unwelcome suitors. Henry I, known as "the Good Scholar," was far from unwelcome; Maud's education and her interest in music made her a good partner for him. However, the question of whether she was a nun had to be settled by a council before she was declared free to marry. Maud's works of mercy earned her the title "Good Queen Maud." She also ruled when Henry was at war.

The embalmed body of **Eleanor of Castile*** (1244–1290), the beloved queen of Edward I, lies on the north side of the chapel, in the tomb of Purbeck marble topped by a gilt-bronze effigy. Strictly speaking, Eleanor was buried in pieces. Her entrails were laid to rest in Lincoln Cathedral and her heart at the Blackfriars Monastery in London, but both of those monuments have since vanished.

The ancient stone screen on the west side of the chapel (on the wall above the coronation chair) was carved in the mid-fifteenth century, and depicts events in the life of St. Edward. The panel on the far left shows the nobles swearing fealty to Queen **Emma** in the name of her unborn son. Emma, also called Aelgifu, was wife to Aethelred and mother to Edward the Confessor. She was a politically minded woman, switching her loyalty from son to son as seemed most likely to serve her purpose. For a long time she advanced the claims of Harthacnut, her son by the Danish conqueror Cnut, to rule England, and she seized the royal treasure and regalia—then at Winchester—in his name. But his stepbrother Harold (Cnut's son from another marriage) took over, and Emma was expelled from England. After Harold's death, Emma and Harthacnut crossed the Channel with sixty ships, but they were unable to secure the English throne. Emma attempted a reconciliation with Edward shortly before he came to power, but he was not impressed and confiscated his mother's wealth soon after he began his reign.

The black marble tomb on the south side of the chapel holds **Philippa of Hainault*** (1314–1369), queen of Edward III. The painted and gilded alabaster effigy is probably a portrait. Her dying wish was that Edward, when he died, would be buried with her at Westminster Abbey. The king spent immense sums of money on her tomb, once surrounded by figures known as weepers which represented those who mourned her. The lady holding a monkey, protected by grille work, is the only one that remains.

After you leave the Confessor's Chapel on its south side, you may want to visit the Chapel of St. Nicholas (two shallow steps), wherein may be seen an enormous memorial strewn with tiny Latin, showing recumbent figures in bright red robes. This was erected by Lord Burghley to his second wife, **Mildred Cecil** (c. 1589), and their daughter **Anne,** Countess of Oxford (d. 1588). Mildred was renowned for her learning and her philanthropy. Another impressive monument in the chapel is the one to **Anne,** Duchess of Somerset (d. 1587), who was described as "a mannish, or rather a devilish woman," who was intolerant, proud, and "exceeding subtle and violent." The alabaster effigy of the duchess is much ornamented; note the golden tassels on the pillows.

To the west is the Chapel of St. Edmund (high ledge), where the tomb of **Frances,** Duchess of Suffolk (1517–1559), may be found. She was the unhappy mother of Lady Jane Grey*, who was executed at the Tower of London in 1553. Nearby in an unmarked grave lies her niece, **Margaret,** Countess of Derby (d. 1596), who was imprisoned by Queen Elizabeth on the charge of witchcraft in 1590. When she was released it was on the condition that she live separately from her husband and refrain from approaching the Court.

Poets' Corner and South Choir Aisle

The South Transept is the site of Poets' Corner, perhaps the most famous burial place in the Abbey. However, an awful lot of the people whose names you see here actually left their remains elsewhere, including the few women commemorated.

A floor plaque near the bookstall commemorates **George Eliot*** (1819–1880). Her enormous contribution to English literature was recognized even in her lifetime, but she was denied burial in the Abbey at the time of her death because of her unorthodox religious beliefs and her longtime, unmarried liaison with George Lewes. Even the agnostic T. H. Huxley thought burial at the Abbey was a poor idea, pointing out that Eliot's "life and opinions were in notorious antagonism to Christian practice in regard to marriage. One cannot have one's cake and eat it too." She was buried instead in Highgate Cemetery, near Lewes.

Near the entrance to St. Faith's Chapel you will find a statue of Shakespeare, and on either side of it is affixed a small wall plaque, one to **Jane Austen*** (1775–1817), who is buried in Winchester Cathedral, and one to **Charlotte***, **Emily,** and **Anne Brontë***. Look carefully to find the plaques, which are dwarfed by the busts of eminent men that hang over them.

In the South Choir Aisle lies a floor plaque to **Sybil Thorndike** (1882–1976), the actress. Known for her great versatility, Thorndike played Shakespearean heroines, tragic Greeks, and high-spirited comic parts. George Bernard Shaw's *St. Joan* was written for her, and she performed it thousands of times. Thorndike also played in motion pictures, making her film debut as Nurse Edith Cavell* in *Dawn* in 1927. She became Dame Sybil Thorndike in 1931.

Over the door to the organ loft is a memorial to Samuel and **Henrietta Octavia Weston Barnett*** (1851–1936), who spent so many years trying to improve social conditions in the East End. Like most reformers, Henrietta had her own way of doing things, and once abducted an eleven-year-old child who was living with her mother in a brothel and had the child placed with friends in the country.

The Cloisters and Pyx Chamber

If you enter the East Cloister from the South Choir Aisle, the first floor slab you come to will be the one marking the burial site of **Aphra Behn*** (1640?–1689), the prolific playwright and novelist of the Restoration. (You may have to work a little to make out the couplet that accompanies her name.) In *A Room of One's Own*, Virginia Woolf wrote of her, "All women together should let flowers fall on the tomb of Aphra Behn . . . for it was she who earned them the right to speak their minds."

A bit farther on you'll find the grave of actress **Anne Bracegirdle*** (1663?–1748), which is somewhat easier to read. Bracegirdle was a belle of the Restoration stage, a beautiful woman who was equally popular in comedies and tragedies. Some of Congreve's works were written especially for her. Her career was eventually eclipsed by the popularity of Anne Oldfield*, however, and she retired at age forty-four.

To see the Pyx Chamber you must pay a separate admission (which also entitles you to see the Chapter House and its museum), but if you're interested in medieval history you may find it worthwhile. The tiled floor of what was once the monastic treasury dates from the thirteenth century. The chamber still houses a huge, ancient chest which once was filled with gold bullion. In medieval times it also contained detailed records of Jewish business transactions, almost certainly including the records of **Licoricia,** widow of David of Oxford. Licoricia was one of the most powerful financiers of her day, and some of the building of the Abbey was accomplished with her money.

By the time you've left your flowers for Aphra Behn and your oats for St. Uncumber, you'll probably be ready to shake off the gloom of tombs and emerge into the daylight once more, where women are still making history.

11

St. James's

Begin and End: Charing Cross Tube Station

St. James's, which fits neatly into the right angle formed by the boundaries of the two parks—Green and St. James's—was originally an area tenanted by those who had connections at court. Whitehall Palace, used by Charles II, was nearby, and St. James's Palace, favored by the eighteenth-century Hanoverians, is within the district itself. Today its precincts are associated with genteel commerce, gentlemen's clubs, and men's furnishings. But a number of women, royal, notorious, or eccentric, have also had their way in St. James's.

From Charing Cross head southwest, passing Northumberland Avenue and Whitehall, and walk through the immense, triple-arched Admiralty Arch to find yourself in a broad avenue known simply as the Mall. The original Mall was built in the reign of Charles II for the purpose of playing pall mall (or paille malle), the croquetlike game which became so popular in his reign. The road was surfaced in cockleshells for better play. The Mall was also a fashionable promenade where society folk strolled in the evening to show off their finery and exchange greetings with one another. The horse ride in St. James's Park follows the original course of the Mall; the present street was built in 1903 to accommodate modern traffic.

St. James's Park is the beautiful triangle of green on your left. It is the oldest royal park. Once a marsh, it was converted by Henry VIII to bowling alley, tilt yard, and deer park. **Elizabeth I*** (1533–1603) hunted here, and Charles I crossed the park on his way to his execution in Whitehall (not the best use of the acreage), but it took Charles II to extend and cultivate the area. It was during his reign that the canal was created from several small ponds. (Now an amazing variety of colorful waterfowl, from terns to pelicans, inhabit the wrench-shaped lake.) Charles was fond of walking in St. James's Park, but on several occasions he found his strolls there interrupted by one **Elizabeth Hooton,** an old woman who followed him about wherever he went— from tennis courts to Whitehall—crying out, "I wait for justice of thee, oh King!" Hooton was a Quaker, who by this time in her life had had many adventures. She was frequently imprisoned for interrupting church services by speaking when the Spirit moved her (perhaps as a result of this she was, like most Friends, a fierce advocate of prison reform). At age sixty she travelled to the New World in order to bring the Quaker message to colonists there, for which labor she was rewarded with flogging and banishment. The letters of petition that she presented to Charles II sought his permission to buy a house and land in one of the British colonies, and the king at last granted this modest request, but Hooton didn't find the colonists much more friendly when she came with a royal certificate than when she had come without one. In 1671 she began her third and final trip to the New World, accompanying the Quaker founder George Fox to the West Indies. She died in Jamaica.

Some years later, **Letitia Pilkington*** (1712–1750) wandered in the park when the lime trees were in flower and considered drowning herself in Rosamond's Pond. Pilkington was a diminutive woman who was genteel but not quite refined, a passionate scribbler, and a friend of Swift. She had been abandoned by her husband and was living in great poverty. In 1748 she was sent to debtor's prison, but was released with the help of the playwright Colley Cibber. She wracked her brains for recollections of Swift: Memories were worth money. But in spite of the success of her memoirs, she died only two years after their publication.

If you'd been sitting in the park on June 29, 1785, you might have been conked on the head by the debris of the lunch eaten by **Letitia Sage.** Mrs. Sage was riding in a hot air balloon, engineered by the Italian Vincent Lunardi and financed by one George Biggin. The flight had been intended to carry four passengers, but in the end the balloon had only lift enough for Mrs. Sage and Mr. Biggin, neither of whom had ever been airborne before. Mr. Biggin operated the balloon, while Mrs. Sage jotted down her impressions in a notebook she had brought along for that purpose; these were later published as "A Letter to a Female Friend." They ate their lunch of chicken, ham, and wine while floating over St. James's Park, and threw the remains—including the empty bottle—over the side.

Much has been made by some authors of the fact that Letitia Sage weighed some two hundred pounds, but in fact, this was not the first time that a Lunardi balloon had failed to lift off with its full roster of passengers. Mr. Biggin's weight, naturally, is not given. (In 1850 Mrs. Margaret Graham, who weighed two hundred and twenty pounds, began ballooning with her three daughters. Mr. Graham was much criticized for allowing his wife to be so headstrong.)

Leave the park where the bridge crosses the canal, and take *Marlborough Road* north between the old dark brick of St. James's Palace on the left and Marlborough House on the right. The latter was built for **Sarah Churchill*** (1660–1744), the Duchess of Marlborough, on a site given her by her close friend, Queen Anne. Sarah laid the foundation stone herself in 1709, and though Sir Christopher Wren had been hired for the job, she fired him before it was done and supervised the building herself. The red brick of Marlborough House was brought from Holland, where Sarah's husband the duke was busy winning battles for England. The Churchills had great influence on royal policy during the days of Sarah's intimate friendship with Queen **Anne*** (1665–1714), who lived next door. The two women called each other Mrs. Freeman and Mrs. Morely, in order to avoid the inequality inherent in the forms of royal address, and Anne was delighted—at first—that Sarah dispensed with obsequiousness and spoke her mind freely. But at last she became irritated by her friend's tactlessness and her blatant Whiggery. Sarah was deposed by a new favorite, **Abigail Hill Masham*** (1670?–1734), who settled for favors for her friends and family, and didn't try to meddle with national affairs.

Turn left into *Pall Mall*, staying on the left-hand side of the street and walking past the brightly-dressed officers who guard the northern face of St. James's Palace. The Palace is on the site of a hospital for fourteen "leprous maidens" which stood here in medieval times. (The lepers used to feed their hogs in the marsh that is now St. James's Park.) The Palace was built by Henry VIII, but only the gatehouse at the south end survives from that first structure; most of the present building dates from 1814. It was after the destruction of the Whitehall Palace by fire, in 1698, that St. James's became the chief royal residence. Both Queen Anne and her older sister, **Mary II*** (of William-and-Mary) (1662–1694), were born here, and **Mary I*** (1516–1558), daughter of Henry VIII and Catherine of Aragon*, died here. The Palace was the scene of the wedding of George IV and his queen **Caroline of Brunswick***, in 1795. Caroline later claimed that her husband was so drunk on his wedding night that he collapsed into the fireplace of the bridal chamber and lay there until morning.

The Palace has not been used as a royal residence since 1820.

After crossing St. James's Street, Pall Mall narrows to continue as *Cleveland Row*, and at its head are several large historic houses. One of these stands on the site of a house given by Charles II to one of his mistresses, **Barbara Villiers** (1640–1709). Villiers—Charles gave her the title Duchess of Cleveland, and the street is named for her—managed to stay in favor long after her tenure as "chief mistress" was over. She was politically and financially shrewd, but like many gamblers, superstitious. For awhile she kept the writer **Mary Delariviere Manley*** (1663–1724) with her because she believed Manley brought her good luck at cards. However, Manley was dismissed within the year for having seduced Villiers' son. She was replaced as mascot by Madame

Beauclair, a kitchen maid who often made gaming her livelihood, and who, according to reports, spoke broken English in a pretense of being French-born.

Retrace your steps to *St. James's Street* and turn left. The street, now commercial, was once celebrated for its chocolate houses, and it was opposite White's Chocolate House that **Letitia Pilkington*** once lodged. At this time in her life she was a bookseller, and also offered to write letters on any subject (except the law) for 12p., ready money. The gentlemen in the window across the street drank to her health and once sent over a bottle of Burgundy.

Next to Locke & Co., on the right-hand side of the street, is Byron House, which stands on the site of a house once occupied by **Ada Lovelace** (1815–1852), Lord Byron's daughter. Lovelace never met her famous father, but she may have found her mother sufficiently interesting. Lady **Noel Byron*** (1792–1860) was a philanthropist of progressive views who ran a children's school. The New England Quaker Lucretia Mott*, who visited the school in 1840, called it "an experiment answering well."

Lovelace herself was a sort of precomputer computer wizard; she worked with Charles Babbage on his "difference" and "analytical" engines, and translated pertinent works from French. Alas, she wasted much of her mathematical genius trying to devise a system of predicting the outcome of horse races, and piled up formidable debts. The programming language ADA, which was developed by the U.S. Department of Defense in 1977, is named for her.

Continue along St. James's Street until *St. James's Place* intersects on its left-hand side. It was on this street that **Hester Chapone*** (1727–1801) and **Mary Delany*** (1700–1788), both Bluestocking intellectuals of the eighteenth century, once lived. Chapone was admired for her sheer audacity. It was remarked that she had the courage to argue with Dr. Johnson, and the novelist Samuel Richardson called her "a little spit-fire." She was married for nine months to the attorney John Chapone, with whom she was very much in love, but after his early death she dedicated herself to intellectual pastimes and to her close friendships with women. Mrs. Delany was a letter-writer and diarist, but was probably best known for the paper mosaic works of flowers and plants which she produced. She began making them when she was seventy-four years old and quit ten years later when her eyesight failed; in that time she produced almost a thousand specimens. Her works were praised by Charles Darwin.

Back in St. James's Street have a look at No. 25, the Economist Building, with its three hexagonal towers in their own raised piazza. It was built in 1964 to designs by the architects Peter and **Alison Smithson** (b. 1928). In addition to designing (with her husband) some of the most influential postwar buildings in England, Smithson has written works on architecture, as well as a novel.

Backtrack to King Street and turn left (east), following it to *St. James's Square*. On your left as you enter the square is a large white building that is now Nos. 16 and 17. It stands on the site of the house in which Queen **Caroline of Brunswick*** (1768–1821) lived during her "trial." Caroline's marriage to her cousin, later George IV, which began so unhappily in St. James's Palace, did not get any better. The two separated a few months after the birth of their child, apparently because George was repelled by Caroline's person. She travelled extensively and engaged in liaisons which may or may not have been adulterous, but which were certainly indiscreet. Upon her husband's accession to the throne in 1820, she returned from abroad to claim her rights as queen. The government offered her an annuity of £50,000 to relinquish her title and remain in exile, but she refused. There followed an investigation by the House of Lords into the question of whether she had committed adultery with one Bartolomeo Bergami. Support for Caroline ran high among the English people, who were disgusted with their king. Every day as she left her home for the trial, people crowded St. James's Square, climbing onto the roofs of carriages for a glimpse of their maligned queen, or renting standing space in carters' wagons for a shilling a day. The queen was acquitted by the House of Lords but was still forcibly excluded from the coronation at Westminster Abbey in July of 1821. She died a few weeks afterward.

In the northeast corner of the square is No. 4, a dark brick building which was once the residence of Lord and Lady Astor. **Nancy Astor*** (1879–1964) was the first woman, and for several years the only woman, to sit in Parliament. She interested herself particularly in the welfare of women and children, and strongly favored tighter controls on the sale of alcohol. The first bill introduced into Parliament by a woman was her bill, introduced in 1923, to prohibit the sale of alcohol in bars to persons under the age of eighteen. In spite of the fact that she married into the English aristocracy (she was from a wealthy Virginian family) she was once quoted as saying: "I married beneath me. All women do."

From the square, take the Duke of York Street north into *Jermyn Street*, which has generally masculine associations with gentlemen's clubs and men's clothing. Here you'll find the brick and stone church of St. James's, Piccadilly. The church was built by Wren in 1684, and restored after bomb damage in World War II. In the barrel-vaulted interior you'll find on the left-hand side of the church, quite near to the front, a memorial plaque to **Mary Delany***. The tablet recounts her marriage history but does not include the fact that her first husband, Pendarves, was an unattractive man of nearly sixty to whom she was married against her will when she was seventeen. To her relief, he died when she was twenty-five. She had a much happier, midlife marriage to Patrick Delany, whom she married against the advice of her family and friends. The tablet praises her "singular ingenuity," the only possible reference to the six volumes of letters and autobiography she left behind when she died. Mrs. Delany had her finger in a lot of pies; it was she who obtained for the novelist Fanny Burney* her place at Queen Charlotte's* court—a post which Burney hated and eventually relinquished.

Also buried in St. James's, Piccadilly, though the site is unmarked, is the portrait painter **Mary Beale*** (1623–1699), who lived in Pall Mall for some time. The daughter of a Suffolk clergyman, she first had her studio in Covent Garden and became noted particularly as a portraitist of intellectuals and churchmen. Her subjects included Charles II and Milton.

Return to St. James's Square and glance east into *Charles II*

Mary Beale

Street, where, beginning in 1773, **Anne Sancho** and her husband
Ignatius kept a grocer shop. Ignatius, who was born on a slave
ship, was given an English education and was a prolific writer
of letters and essays, as well as the friend of many authors and
artists of his day. His letters, collected and edited after his death
by Miss **Crewe,** reveal that Anne may have been something of
an herbalist. "Mrs. Sancho would send you some tamarinds," he
wrote to one friend in 1777. "I know not her reasons; as I hate

contentions, I contradicted not—but shrewdly suspect she thinks you want cooling." Tamarind pods were believed by herbalists to be an effective purge of choler (anger). Anne, who was from the West Indies, bore six children. She continued to keep shop after her husband's death.

From St. James's Square, go south to *Pall Mall* and turn right. Pall Mall was laid out in 1661 and originally called Catherine Street, after **Catherine of Braganza** (1638–1705), queen to Charles II. But from the beginning it was nicknamed for the mallet game the king was so fond of playing with his courtiers and mistresses. The street was initially a very fashionable address, and glittered with the mansions of the rich and titled. Toward the end of the eighteenth century a great many writers and artists moved into the area, changing its character somewhat.

On the left-hand side of the street you'll find Nos. 80–82, known as Schomberg House. The miniature painter **Maria Cosway** (flourished 1820) once lived at No. 80 with her husband, the painter Richard Cosway. Although Cosway's birthdate is not known, one gruesome detail of her childhood is available: Her nurse murdered four of her brothers and sisters in order to facilitate their road to heaven. Cosway was born in Florence of an English or Irish father and studied in Rome under Fuseli and others. She wanted to be a nun, but after her father's death her mother brought her to England, where she began her career as a miniaturist, using chiefly mythological subjects. She was a successful artist and exhibited many times at the Royal Academy. Her marriage to Richard Cosway seems to have been less successful than her career; he kept her secluded when they first married because of her "foreign" manners, and in later years they frequently lived apart.

Next door, at No. 79 (now the Peninsular and Oriental Steam Navigation Company), a plaque relates that **Nell Gwynne*** (1650–1687) lived in a house on this site. Without a doubt the most fascinating of Charles II's many mistresses, frank, reckless, generous Nell was enormously popular with the English people. She was born and bred in poverty, but her illiteracy did not impair her wit, and when she rose to wealth and splendor she never forgot her old friends. One anecdote that demonstrates her strong-willed ways recounts that in 1676, determined to secure a title for her six-year-old son by Charles, she dangled him by his heels out a window, threatening to drop him, until the alarmed Charles cried out, "Save the Earl of Burford!"

Reverse your direction and take Pall Mall east to *Waterloo Place*, a broad street-cum-parking lot dotted with statues. To your left you'll see **Florence Nightingale*** (1820–1910) upon a pedestal, holding a lamp. That lamp, which has become her symbol, was not, in fact, the sort she carried. Turn right into Waterloo Place, crossing to the left-hand side of the street in order to pass the marvellous statue of polar explorer Captain Robert Scott sculpted by his wife, later Lady **Kathleen Kennet*** (1878–1947). She was already a sculptor when they married in 1908. He sailed for the Antarctic two years later, and she was on a ship bound for New Zealand, in order to meet him, when she heard of his death. She turned her energy to her art, and the statue of her husband which stands before you is her first masterwork. After she married the politician Hilton Young (later Lord Kennet) in 1922, her duties as a political hostess slowed down her artistic career.

At the end of Waterloo Place a staircase leads down to the Mall, from which you can return to Charing Cross Station through the Admiralty Arch. (Those in wheelchairs can go north on Waterloo Place, turn right [east] into Pall Mall, then jog right on Cockburn Street and follow it to Charing Cross.)

12
Mayfair

Begin: Piccadilly Circus Tube Station
End: Oxford Street Tube Station

Between 1700 and 1750 the bluest bloods of London moved west into Mayfair. They kicked out the highwaymen and footpads and turned the area into the smartest, most fashionable, most expensive place to live, and Mayfair may still be that, though the residents cough up their millions for flats instead of mansions now. Mayfair is also famous for its shopping—Bond Street and the nearly impassable Oxford Street are at its very heart, and Regent Street, also famous for its shops, forms its eastern boundary. Selfridge's, Dickins and Jones, Liberty's, Swan and Edgar's, and Cartier's are a few of the marketplaces Mayfair boasts; within its precincts one can buy clothing, jewelry, autographs, and art.

But the walk that follows skirts Mayfair's renowned emporiums and glittering specialty shops, taking you on quieter streets past sites often associated with artists and intellectuals. However much money they may have had—and some of them did, though some of them didn't—it is not for their wealth that they are remembered.

From Piccadilly Circus head west on *Piccadilly* itself (across Regent Street from Lillywhites) passing Sackville Street and continuing on until you come to a massive facade on your right-hand side hung with a line of Union Jacks. This is Burlington House, home of the Royal Academy of Arts†. The building dates back to 1600, but substantial changes were made in the early eighteenth century and in 1867, when it was converted to its present use.

On the left-hand side of the courtyard as you enter are the offices of several scholarly societies, including the Royal Astronomical Society. In 1828 the Society awarded **Caroline Herschel*** (1750–1848) a gold medal to honor her astronomical discoveries; they also published two of her papers. Herschel was from a musically talented German family, and when she first came to England to join her brother William, she attempted a career as a singer. She had already given up that idea by the time that William took up astronomy, and she happily became his assistant when he was appointed court astronomer to George III. Her first independent discovery took place on August 1, 1786, when she sighted a new comet, and over the next few decades she continued to make significant contributions to the field of astronomy. In 1835, when she was eighty-five years old, the Royal Astronomical Society made her an honorary member. She was never given full membership, of course.

On the same occasion that it awarded honorary membership to Herschel, the Society bestowed the same privilege on **Mary Somerville** (1780–1872), the Scottish mathematician and astronomer. Somerville's early passion for science horrified her mother, and she used to study secretly by sewing during her brother's lessons. In 1826 Somerville presented a paper to the Royal Astronomical Society; she continued to write on scientific subjects all her life. Her book on molecular and microscopic science was published when she was ninety-two. Somerville's is the first signature on the petition for women's suffrage presented to Parliament by John Stuart Mill in 1866.

Nearby is the headquarters of the Society of Antiquaries, which in 1954 chose the archaeologist **Joan Evans** (1893–1977) to be its first woman director. Evans wrote over thirty works on archaeology and literature, specializing in the medieval period in France and writing a great deal about the jewelry of the era.

The Royal Academy of Arts itself has a mixed history regarding women. On the one hand, there were two women among its founding members in 1768. One of these was **Mary Moser*** (1744–1819), flower painter and intimate of the royal family. Moser started her career early, giving her first show when she was fourteen. Employed by Queen Charlotte*, she was paid over £900 to decorate a chamber at Frogmore, which the queen then named "Miss Moser's Room." At the age of fifty-three Moser married a military officer and gave up the professional practice of her art.

The other woman who was a founding member of the Academy was **Angelica Kauffmann*** (1741–1807), the neoclassic and history painter. Some of the ceiling paintings in the hall on the ground floor of Burlington House are hers: Note especially the wonderful depiction of a woman sketching on the far left side of the ceiling as you enter. These paintings were originally in the Academy's home at Somerset House.

After getting off to such a good start, the RA proceeded to give women a lot of grief. Women were not allowed in RA schools until 1861, when **Laura Herford** (1831–1870) gained admission to classes by submitting work signed with her initials only. Once the RA found that it had admitted a woman, it permitted four other women to join the class, though none was allowed to draw from nude models. By this time, of course, many male artists were disdaining the Royal Academy schools, which they believed were too bound by convention and tradition. Still, such distinguished artists as **Barbara Hepworth*** (1903–1975) and **Vanessa Bell*** (1879–1961) studied at the RA.

The Academy has not always been equitable even to its members. Dame **Laura Knight*** (1877–1970), though made a full member in 1936, was not allowed to attend the annual members' banquet until 1967, thirty-one years later. Knight had a special attraction to circuses and gypsies, and painted many pictures on these subjects.

Among the many women who have exhibited at the RA is

Lady **Elizabeth Thompson Butler** (1850–1933), who specialized in military subjects. In 1874 her painting *Calling the Role After an Engagement* created such a sensation that the crowds had to be controlled by policemen. But she failed by two votes to be elected to the Academy.

Continue west on Piccadilly a few blocks (passing Bond Street) until you come to *Dover Street* on your right. Before turning in, pause to admire the sculpture *Horse and Rider* by **Elizabeth Frink*** (b. 1930). The naked man upon his horse makes an interesting contrast to standard equestrian statues. No. 40, on the left-hand side of Dover Street, was once the home of Lady **Stanley,** Bertrand Russell's maternal grandmother. Russell remembered her as an active, opinionated old woman who was fond of saying: "I have left my brain to the Royal College of Surgeons, because it will be so interesting for them to have a clever woman's brain to cut up." No. 40 was of course also the home of **Kate Stanley** (1842–1874), later Lady Amberley, before she married Russell's father. Lady Amberley circulated petitions for women's suffrage and lectured publicly for the cause as early as 1870, attracting much disapproval. Queen Victoria* herself said sternly that "Lady Amberley ought to get a *good whipping.*"

Return to Piccadilly and continue west until you reach *Stratton Street* on your right (by now you will have the vast diamond of Green Park on your left). For many years **Angela Burdett-Coutts*** (1814–1906), the one woman in the chapter who is indeed remembered for her wealth, or at least for her generous disposal of it, lived at the head of Stratton Street. Angela came to live here when she inherited the vast fortune which began her career in philanthropy and wandered among the damask draperies, gilded mirrors, and marble busts feeling a bit overwhelmed. However, she soon settled into serious giving and occupied herself with her myriad works of mercy until the age of sixty-six, when her fortune was much reduced by her marriage to a North American half her age. (By the terms of the inheritance, marriage to an alien gave other relations claims upon the estate.) However, the marriage lasted twenty-seven years and apparently made her very happy.

Angela's efforts on behalf of working people made her enormously popular; she was called "The Queen of the Poor" and hailed wherever she went. In December of 1866, thousands of working men marched along Piccadilly en route to a huge demonstration in favor of franchise reform. As they passed her house and saw her figure in the bow window, cheers rang out, again and again, for over two hours as the men moved past. They cheered in memory of her father, who had in his own time worked for the first Reform Bill, but they also cheered for her, because of her work in the East End and among the poor everywhere.

An address in *Piccadilly* was the site of the brutal and exploitive treatment of **Saartjie Baartman,** who was called "the Hottentot Venus" on advertising leaflets. Baartman was born in the interior of Africa but grew up near the Cape, being sold into slavery by Boers who gave her a Dutch name. She served as a nursery-maid in the home of Henrick Caesar, who brought her to London in 1810 and charged people money to see her. Baartman had a figure which was "distorted beyond all European notions of beauty," including especially protuberant buttocks. Caesar advertised that she was the epitome of beauty among the Hottentot (Khoikhoi) people, and accommodated parties of twelve or more with private exhibitions in which Baartman stood on a stage, clothed in a dress the same color as her skin, and was made to walk, stand, dance, sit, come and go, according to her keeper's orders. All this she did with great sullenness, and when she grew tired he took a stick to her. She was believed to have been about twenty-six at this time; she had been married at the Cape and had born a child, who did not live.

In 1810 the slave trade had been abolished for three years, and concerned citizens hearing about the goings-on in Piccadilly soon brought an inquiry. Dutch interpreters were secured, as Baartman knew only a little English, and the interrogators, of course, were unfamiliar with her native tongue. Baartman told the investigators that she had come to England of her own consent, for a term of six years, and was to have half the profits from the show. In fact, after eighteen months in London Caesar traded her to a Parisian animal-showman, and she eventually died in Paris, without ever having seen any "profits." Baartman was described as having a sprightly personality and a good memory; she was fluent in Dutch and knew a little English and French. Her final illness may have been alcohol-related.

From Piccadilly, turn right (north) on narrow *Bolton Street*, where modern buildings stare across at the older ones. You'll have to stand across the street from it to see the plaque on No. 11, where **Fanny Burney*** (1752–1840) once lived. The plaque calls her Madame D'Arblay, but she didn't acquire that name until 1793, when, at age forty-one, she married a French exile. By then she had already written a number of successful novels and plays, though her play *The Witlings*, which satirized her Blues-tocking friends, was never produced.

At the north end of Bolton Street, turn left into Curzon Street, and wander past the shops until you come to *Queen Street* on your right. This was once the home of the courtesan **Harriette Wilson** (d. 1846?), who in 1825 published her memoirs which recounted scandalous anecdotes about many of the prominent men who had been her lovers. She wasn't shy about naming names, though she did allow the men in question to buy them-selves out of the book ahead of time, if they so chose. The Duke of Wellington's famous answer was "Publish and be damned." Wilson explained to her past paramours that she was not so young and desirable as she had once been, and needed the money the sale of the memoirs—which were popular indeed—would bring her.

Wilson took a dim view of society's reliance on chastity as a foundation for other virtues: "She is a bad woman the moment she has committed fornication, be she generous, charitable, just, clever, domestic, affectionate, and ever ready to sacrifice her own good to benefit those she loves. . . ." she complained. "[Yet] all are virtuous who are chaste, even when chastity is to their liking, or when they are entirely destitute of affections or natural passion."

Continue west on Curzon Street until you come to *South Audley Street*, then turn right (north). The street was once the very fashionable address of a number of aristocrats, including Lord Bute, who had two women sent to Bridewell in 1763 for singing political ballads outside his door. The fourth street on your left will be *South Street*. Turn left and proceed west toward Hyde Park. No. 15, on the right-hand side of the street, bears a plaque to **Catherine Walters** (1839–1920), "the last Victorian courtesan," who once lived here. Walters, who was known as Skittles, was famed for her good horsemanship and for her coarse language, both of which she practiced freely in nearby Hyde Park.

On the opposite side of the street, straddling two buildings (one of which is quite modern), is a plaque which reads: "In a house on this site **Florence Nightingale***, 1820–1910, lived and died." Nightingale is best known for her remarkable achievements in the Crimean War. In 1854 she supervised a staff of thirty-eight nurses at the front, and as a result of the hygienic practices she initiated, the death rate in the medical units fell from 42 percent to 2.2 percent.

Retrace your steps and turn left onto *South Audley Street*, continuing north. In a block you will come to charming Grosvenor Chapel, a small, eighteenth-century building the walls of which are studded with memorial tablets. Both Lady **Mary Wortley Montagu*** (1689–1762) and **Elizabeth Carter*** (1717–1806) are buried here in unmarked graves. Montagu was perhaps best known for her letters about Turkey, where she travelled with her husband, and for her vigorous efforts to have the Turkish practice of innoculation against smallpox adopted in England. Carter was probably the most intellectual of all the Bluestockings; her translations of Epictetus were much admired. She was determined not to marry, and grew quite exasperated with the matchmaking schemes of her friends. When first introduced to **Catherine Talbot** (d. 1770), however, her feelings were quite different. "Miss Talbot is my passion," she wrote to an acquaintance. "I think of her every day, dream of her all night, and one way or another introduce her into every subject I talk of." Their friendship lasted thirty years, until Talbot's death.

Before you leave, it's worthwhile having a prowl around the church to survey some of the tablets of the "ordinary" wives, mothers, and sisters who are here commemorated. And if you want to rest for a moment before continuing on, the gardens behind the chapel are lovely.

Continue north on South Audley Street until you reach Grosvenor Square, a six-acre expanse of green sometimes called "Little America" from a variety of associations with the United States. The entire west side of the square is occupied by the U.S. Embassy, and the park itself includes a monument to Franklin Delano Roosevelt, erected by the English in 1948. Cut through the square to its northeast corner and travel several blocks east on Brook Street until you arrive at *Hanover Square*.

In 1872, an early women's rights meeting was held at the Hanover Square Rooms. Women attending included **Millicent Fawcett*** (1847–1929), **Lydia E. Becker,** and **Ernestine Rose.** Becker (1827–1890) had convened one of the first public women's suffrage meetings in England in 1868. Her early advocacy brought her public scorn and ridicule. The author of a letter to the *Stroud Journal*, who signed himself "A He-Critter," wrote: "I read somewhere the other day that there are now three sexes—masculine, feminine, and Miss Becker. The latter model seems to be popular, and as the latest fashion is the breath of life to a large section of the female world."

Ernestine Rose (1810–1892) was sixty-two at the time of the meeting. A native of Poland, Rose showed her independent spirit at the age of sixteen, when she refused to be married off by her father, a rabbi. She left home a year later and eventually made her way to London, where she was attracted by the Owenite movement and married William Rose, a jeweller and silversmith who was also an Owenite. In 1836 the couple moved to the United States, where Ernestine became one of the founders of the women's rights movement in that country. She was a popular orator on behalf of the women's movement for many years, and when she and her husband retired in London, in 1869, she continued to speak now and then. She is buried next to her husband in Highgate Cemetery.

Take *St. George Street* south from the square until it intersects with Maddox Street. There you'll find the church of St. George's, Hanover Square (steps). The interior of St. George's is more solemn and stately than that of Grosvenor Chapel; it's a highly appropriate environment for weddings and funerals. The wedding of **George Eliot*** (1819–1880) to John Walter Cross, which was held here on May 6, 1880, was a quiet affair. Eliot was by then sixty years old; Cross was forty. There was some surprise that she had married so soon after the death of George Lewes, whom she had called husband for so many years (though they were never married). But Eliot's women friends wished her much joy. Though Eliot herself said frankly that she had never cared much for women, she inspired some deep emotions among members of her sex. The feminist Barbara Bodichon* wrote upon hearing the news: "Tell Johnny Cross I should have done exactly what he has done if you would have let me and I had been a man."

When you leave the church, turn right (west) on Maddox Street, and shortly after crossing Regent Street you will find an alley called *Argyll Street* which leads left, passing behind Dickins and Jones department store. A plaque on the wall of the store commemorates the residence of **Germaine de Stael** (1766–1817) in a house on this site in 1813 and 1814. Madame de Stael, born Germaine Necker, was a French novelist, literary critic, and political writer, known for her scandalous affairs with men and passionate friendships with women. She was married at age twenty to Baron de Stael-Hostein, the Swedish Ambassador to Paris, but the marriage was unhappy, and Madame de Stael took her pleasure from other relationships, including a long-lived friendship with Juliette Recamier. "I love you with a love surpassing that of friendship," Madame de Stael wrote to Juliette. "I go down on my knees to embrace you with all my heart."

De Stael's Paris salons were a meeting place for liberal members of the aristocracy before the French Revolution, but she later found she could not support the revolutionists and fled Paris. She returned in 1795 and reestablished her salon, which became a center of opposition to Napoleon. In 1804 she was exiled by the emperor and was not able to return to Paris until Napoleon's abdication in 1814; it was during this time that she lived in London's Mayfair.

If you continue down Argyll Street you will come to Oxford Street, where you can lose yourself in the dense crowds of shoppers—or escape by diving down the entrance to the tube station on the corner.

13

Marylebone

Begin: Oxford Circus Tube Station
End: Baker Street Tube Station

Like many London neighborhoods, Marylebone was once an independent village, and Marylebone High Street, a charming place to have tea and scones at a sidewalk cafe on a sunny morning, still serves as the "Main Street" for the district. But in the rest of the area no village atmosphere remains: The wide and well-trafficked streets are laid out in a neat grid, and the eighteenth-century buildings that once predominated are now found as remnants among more modern office buildings. Marylebone's associations with women are chiefly domestic ones. Women have lived, scribbled, studied, and quarrelled in the precincts of St. Marylebone, in houses that can be more often remembered than seen.

Among these women was the poet **Elizabeth Barrett Browning*** (1806–1861), who is to Marylebone as Virginia Woolf* is to Bloomsbury. It was here that she lived with her oppressive father, here that she wrote the volumes of poems published when she was in her thirties, here that she secretly married

Elizabeth Barrett Browning

Robert Browning. Following her string of addresses around Marylebone is a fascinating enterprise, but the first Marylebone dwelling you'll see on this walk is associated not with Browning, nor with any literary lady, but with those omnipresent, unquenchable suffragettes.

From the Oxford Circus tube station, go west on Oxford Street (you'll pass John Prince's Street on your right-hand side), and escape the hordes of shoppers by turning right (north) into Holles Street. This will bring you into *Cavendish Square*. On the north side of the circular gardens a columned facade dates back to 1717, but our interest lies in the much more recent building of No. 20, on the west side. It was here, as the Blue Plaque will inform you, that Herbert Henry Asquith lived from 1895 to 1908. On June 19, 1906, a small delegation of suffragettes called upon Asquith to present their demand for the vote; they found him not at home. Two days later a larger delegation, which included about thirty working women from the East End, made a repeat visit. Several women were arrested, including **Theresa Billington-Greig*** (1877–1964), **Annie Kenney*** (1879–1953), and an elderly woman named Mrs. **Sparborough** who supported herself and her husband through needlework. Asquith's position was that he would not deal with any issue not directly related to his office of Chancellor; the suffragettes' position was that since as Chancellor he was responsible for levying taxes on women who had no voice in government, the suffrage issue ought to be very much his concern. Asquith left No. 20 in 1908 to reside at No. 10 Downing Street, but his troubles with the suffragettes were just beginning.

The house was converted to the Cowdray Club for Nurses in the 1920s, and the stone facade and portico you see now date from 1932.

Asquith's years at No. 20 were enlivened by the presence of his second wife, **Margot Tennant** (1864–1945). Raised in Scotland, Tennant was a huntswoman, a society queen, and an intellectual: She belonged to a group called "the Souls" composed of intellectuals and aesthetes who advocated, among other things, greater freedom for women, particularly in self-expression and dress. During her marriage to Asquith she was a brilliant and witty society hostess. In the early 1920s, when her husband had been ousted as Prime Minister by the administration of Lloyd George, Tennant published a candid autobiography which created a sensation in London. She also published essays and travel writing.

An earlier resident of Cavendish Square was Lady **Charlotte Guest** (1812–1895), at that time married to the M.P. Charles Schreiber. Between her first and second marriages, Guest lived in Wales, where she studied Welsh and translated the Welsh legends of *The Mabinogion*. This work, which took her eight years, was published in three volumes between the years 1838 and 1849.

Lady **Mary Wortley Montagu*** (1689–1762) lived on the east side of the square, at No. 5, in the early eighteenth century, after returning from her travels in Turkey where she had accompanied her husband on a diplomatic mission. Lady Mary was most interested in Islamic customs and studied Turkish in order to read the poetry. (The plaque at No. 5 is to a later resident, Quinton Hogg.)

Leave Cavendish Square at its northwest corner and head north on *Harley Street*, famous for its fashionable practitioners of medicine. No. 7, a building of red brick and yellow stone which now houses a firm of solicitors, was once the home of **Clara Butt*** (1873–1937), a powerful contralto who made her London debut at age nineteen. In addition to her renown as a concert artist, Butt was remarkable for her height, being six feet two inches tall. Hers was one of the signatures on a petition given to Prime Minister Lloyd George in 1918, which requested government support for a bill allowing women to practice law.

Also on Harley Street is a plain building with a distinguished history: Queen's College, founded in 1848, is the oldest institution for the higher education of women in England. Its students were from the upper middle class, and its fees were relatively high, but its academic standards were similarly high.

Originally established in order to insure adequate education for those intending to be governesses, it played a crucial role in the development of other women's educational institutions through the training of pioneers in the field. Ironically, Queen's College itself used only male teachers until the twentieth century and did not have a female principal until 1931.

Dorothea Beale (1831–1906) attended lectures at Queen's College soon after it opened its doors. Ten years later she became principal of Cheltenham Ladies' College, and her effect upon it was enormous. She dramatically increased enrollment, reorganized finances, and erected new buildings. In 1893 she founded St. Hilda's Hall, a teacher training institution at Oxford; it later became one of the University colleges.

Frances Buss (1827–1894) concentrated on bringing education to women of modest means. Her father was a printer and her mother ran a school for girls; Buss founded her own school in Camden in 1850, teaching during the day and attending lectures at Queen's College evenings. Her day school, which had low fees and high academic standards, later became the North London Collegiate School. Its curriculum included philosophy, Latin, and science, as well as basic subjects, and after expansion in 1879 included athletics. The school, like a boys' public school, aimed to prepare women for entrance examinations at universities.

Beale and Buss were so strongly identified with the cause of educated women that a derisive public circulated the following jingle about them:

> *Miss Buss and Miss Beale*
> *Cupid's darts do not feel.*
> *How different to us*
> *Are Miss Beale and Miss Buss!*

A somewhat later student at Queen's College who was important in the field of women's education was **Frances Dove** (1847–1942). A younger contemporary described her in her later years as "handsome, erect, white-haired, masterful, more feminist than feminine." After preparation at Queen's College she attended Girton College (later the first women's college at Cambridge), and eventually joined the staff at Cheltenham Ladies' College. Later she founded her own school at Wycombe Abbey, and when suffragists came to speak there, she joined them on the platform, a wagon bed—until the crowd threatened to overturn them all, and the women had to scramble over a wall to escape.

Women of achievement in fields other than education also attended Queen's College. These included **Sophia Jex-Blake*** (1840–1912), one of the women who fought to open the medical profession to women. After a long struggle to study medicine in the United Kingdom, Jex-Blake finally received her medical degree from the University of Bern. But she continued unabated in her efforts on behalf of women medical students, founding her own college for a time. She was the first woman doctor in

Scotland, and it was through her work that the Edinburgh Medical School at last opened its doors to women.

Several prominent writers have also attended Queen's College, among them the fascinating **Gertrude Bell** (1868–1926), explorer and linguist. Bell spent much of her life travelling in the Middle East, learning Arabic, climbing mountains, and writing of her adventures. Another writer who attended Queen's College was the New Zealand short story writer **Katherine Mansfield*** (1888–1923), who arrived when she was fifteen. Almost the first person she encountered was a tall, blond, timid girl named **Ida Constance Baker*** (1888–1978), who for the next twenty years—until Mansfield's death—would be her devoted friend.

When you are done reflecting upon the generations of schoolgirls who have studied at Queen's College, proceed to New Cavendish Street, turn left, then turn right into famous *Wimpole Street*. Tennyson called it a "dark unlovely street"; Virginia Woolf called it "the most august of London streets, the most impersonal." The most famous address on Wimpole Street is No. 50, which bears a round red plaque high on its wall and an additional inscription below eye level, attesting to the fact that **Elizabeth Barrett Browning*** once lived in a house on this site. It was here that Mr. Barrett, father of five, ruled tyranically over his offspring. Though all adult, they were financially dependent upon their father, and he called the shots—no friends allowed for dinner, marriage not even discussable, outings with friends discouraged. Yet Elizabeth was in many ways devoted to her father. They shared deep religious convictions and always prayed together before retiring.

Because Elizabeth was very much of an invalid, the house on Wimpole Street was in many ways her entire world. Her attitude toward it is reflected in a letter to a friend, in which she remarked that the walls of the house "look so much like Newgate [Prison] turned inside out." Through the wide bay windows she had a view of dark houses and chimney pots. The neighborhood was at that time a quiet one. "We live on the verge of the town rather than in it," Elizabeth wrote. "Flush's breathing is my loudest sound, and then the watch's tickings, and then my heart when it beats too turbulently." Flush, of course, was her adored spaniel, whose engaging biography has been written by Virginia Woolf*.

Retreat to New Cavendish Street and turn right (west), then left into *Welbeck Street,* which still contains many eighteenth-century houses. Between Bulstrode and Bentinck streets you will find No. 51, a brick building on the right-hand side of the street which was once the Langham Hotel. Here the novelist Maria Louisa de la Ramée, better known as **Ouida** (1839–1908), lived with her mother for a short time in 1867. Ouida's books were frankly escapist and wildly emotional, but they were also enormously popular.

Elizabeth Barrett Browning* and her husband Robert also lodged in Welbeck Street, on one of their trips back to England from Italy, where they lived most of their married lives. Elizabeth always hoped to be reconciled with her father, but he never forgave her for having defied him to marry Robert Browning. He never spoke to her after her marriage, and he disinherited her. However, she wasn't singled out—he did the same to two more of his children who dared to marry.

From Welbeck Street turn right into Wigmore Street, and follow it past shops and a large IBM building until you reach *Portman Square,* now heavily trafficked and surrounded by modern buildings. In 1781, **Elizabeth Montagu*** (1720–1800), known as the "Queen of the Blues," lived in the square. Montagu's literary salons were attended by Dr. Johnson and Boswell, by Horace Walpole, and of course by other Bluestockings. Montagu also considered herself the patron of London's chimney sweeps, and gave an annual dinner for them at her house featuring roast beef and plum pudding.

The interior of the square, like most in Marylebone, is not open to the public.

From the northwest corner of the square take *Upper Berkeley Street* west. On the north side of the street, in the block between Great Cumberland and Seymour Place, you will find No. 20. A plaque on the house commemorates that pioneer of women's medicine, **Elizabeth Garrett Anderson*** (1836–1917). Anderson's medical education was pieced together from a number of institutions, including St. Andrew's in Scotland, where she dissected cadavers in her room as the dissecting rooms were prohibited to women.

Continue west on Upper Berkeley Street, which becomes Connaught Street after you cross Edgeware Road, and you will shortly arrive at elegant *Connaught Square,* which dates from the 1820s. (We have now strayed into Bayswater.) No. 14, a typical structure of creamy horizontals and dark brick on the east side of the square, is marked with a plaque to show that the Italian ballet dancer **Marie Taglioni** (1804–1884) lived here in 1875 and 1876. Taglioni, who has been described as a "poetic, wistful dancer," was the idol of audiences in Paris, London, and St. Petersburg. After her stage career was over she taught at the Opera in France and coached young ballerinas.

From the northeast corner of the square cross Connaught Street to find yourself in *Portsea Place,* where on the left-hand side of the street you'll see No. 16, marked with a plaque noting the residence of the South African writer and feminist **Olive Schreiner** (1855–1920). Schreiner's autobiographical novel, *Story of an African Farm,* was published under the pseudonym Ralph Iron. Schreiner wrote many essays attacking Christianity and the oppression of women, and worked for racial justice as well as for women's suffrage. In 1894 Schreiner married a South African farmer who shared many of her views. He changed his name to hers upon their marriage and kept her name, in spite of ridicule, even after she died.

Turn right on Kendal Street, recross Edgeware Road, and travel several blocks east on George Street to reach the long, thin strip of garden surrounded by railings that is *Bryanston Square.* Both Bryanston Square and its skinny twin, *Montagu Square,* were built by David Porter, who started life as a chimney sweep. He named the latter after **Elizabeth Montagu*** to honor her patronage of the sweeps.

The church of St. Mary's, Bryanston Square, is not actually in the square. You can reach it by turning left into Bryanston Square from George Street, and continuing north on Wyndham Place until it dead-ends at the church just across Crawford Street. (There are some benches in the little plaza before the church, handy for those who have been looking forward to resting their feet.) The multitiered church with its circular colonnade was built in the 1820s. It was in this parish that the social reformer **Octavia Hill*** (1838–1912) did some of her most important work. Hill was interested in change, not just relief. In an attempt to improve housing, she bought up groups of houses and let them in sets of two rooms each. She collected the rents herself, made sure any necessary repairs were made, and purchased applian-ces for her tenants with money left over from the repair fund. Hill campaigned for the preservation of open space and recrea-tional areas, and was one of the founders of the National Trust in 1895. She was at one time a close friend of the medical pioneer Sophia Jex-Blake*; however, they later quarrelled.

    Henrietta Octavia Weston Barnett* (1851–1936) worked with Hill in the parish, and it was while doing this work that she met Arthur Barnett. After they married, they moved to Whitechapel and continued their efforts at social reform together.

    Turn left (east) on Crawford Street and in a couple blocks you'll reach *Gloucester Place*. Turn left to see the plaque on the corner house, No. 99. You are now in **Elizabeth Barrett Brown-ing*** territory again. This was the first London address the Bar-retts had when they moved from the country, and Elizabeth was not completely charmed by the foul chimneys and muddy streets of London. "We can't see even a leaf or a sparrow without soot on it," she wrote to a friend. She was not yet an invalid at this time in her life—as a child, she climbed trees, played with bows and arrows, and dreamed of riding along the Danube in a suit of steel armor, singing her poems and gathering warriors as she rode. While living at Gloucester Place, she enjoyed seeing the parrots at the zoo and the pictures at the Royal Academy. But she did not neglect her work. She had already published two books of poetry by the time they moved to London in 1835, and she continued her career by writing a long religious poem called "The Seraphim."

    Turn tail and head south on Gloucester Place (crossing Craw-ford Street), then turn left into *Dorset Street*. Elizabeth and Robert Browning lodged at No. 13 in 1855, on one of their trips to London from Italy, and were almost overwhelmed by all their visitors. Elizabeth was extremely interested in spiritualism at this time, an interest of which Robert strongly disapproved. Elizabeth herself did not always find the mediums she visited convincing.

It was the following year that Elizabeth's narrative poem *Aurora Leigh* was published. Though sometimes dismissed today as sentimental, at the time of its publication the book was both extremely popular and quite controversial. Readers who felt poetry should be "pretty" were disturbed by references to streetwalkers, sweat, and the coupling of beasts, and by the use of verbs such as "stink." *Aurora Leigh* makes strong claims for women's freedom, women's work, and married love.

Turn left (north) on Baker Street, then (after several highly commercial blocks) right into *Marylebone Road*. You can't miss the Madame Tussaud's Waxworks†—look for the long lines of tourists waiting to get in, then look on the wall above their heads to see the medallion-type portrait of the woman who started it all.

Marie Tussaud (1761–1850) began modelling figures for her uncle, Philippe Curitus, in Paris in 1780. By the time of the French revolution, they had a thriving business between them. In 1789 both uncle and niece "proved" that they were patriots, but later they lost their credibility, and the uncle was sent to the guillotine in 1794. Marie herself was imprisoned for three months but was then released. She took death masks of many guillotine victims, and after her marriage in 1795 to engineer Francis Tussaud, she emigrated to England in 1802 with the remnants of her wax collection. For the next thirty-three years she gave exhibitions in London and toured the provinces with her ever-expanding show.

Today in addition to its original treasures, including a death mask of the French queen **Marie Antoinette*** (1755–1793) which is in the Chamber of Horrors, the museum includes historical tableaux, such as **Mary,** Queen of Scots* (1524–1587) at her execution, and a scene of the **Brontë*** sisters sitting for their portrait. The wax statues of famous celebrities range from **Agatha Christie** (1890–1976) to **Indira Gandhi** (1917–1984).

Across Marylebone Road from the museum, and a couple of blocks east of it, is the St. Marylebone Parish Church. The present structure with its massive columns dates only from the nineteenth century, but there has been a church on this site since about 1400. It was here that Elizabeth Barrett and Robert Browning were secretly married. A cabinet on the church porch displays a facsimile of the marriage register and pictures of the way the church looked at the time. (There is a ramp to the right of the church for those who cannot climb the stairs.) Within the church, the *Browning Room* has a stained glass window commemorating the wedding and a shelf of books including works by both Brownings. However, the room is often locked, and is best viewed by appointment (call 01-935 7315).

Elizabeth and Robert originally met by mail, but by the time they married Robert had paid some ninety visits to the invalid genius in her room. Elizabeth's decision to defy her revered father and to give up everything she knew must have taken tremendous courage, for she had few resources of her own—not even her health.

On the morning of September 12, 1846, Elizabeth and her maid Wilson left the house at Wimpole Street and went by cab to the St. Marylebone Parish Church. Robert Browning met his bride at the door, and after the ceremony they parted there. Elizabeth returned home that afternoon as though nothing had happened and kept her monumental secret for another week. At the end of that time, she and Browning left with Wilson and the spaniel Flush for Italy, not daring even to say goodbye to her father. They spent most of their married lives there and became deeply involved in the cause of Italian unification.

Elizabeth Barrett Browning wrote poetry all her life, though by many she has been remembered chiefly for the romance of her clandestine marriage. For some, too, she has become a symbol of hope, a promise that it is never too late to break even those bonds which we have been taught to cherish.

Across Marylebone Road from the church is York Gate, which will lead you to Regent's Park. From 1935 to 1952 the Anglo-Irish novelist **Elizabeth Bowen** (1899–1973) lived in this neighborhood, and several of her books include vivid descriptions of the park. Her novels feature precise psychological portraits of characters engaged in confronting the moral issues of the twentieth century. *The Heat of the Day* paints a vivid picture of life in London during World War II.

Regent's Park itself comprises 487 acres of greenery and boasts gardens, canals, a boating lake, an open-air theater, and the London Zoological Gardens. It's a marvellous place to play, and when you're done, you can return by bus (#74 goes to and from the zoo). Or, if you haven't strayed too far from York Gate, you can return to Marylebone Road and pop down the Baker Street tube station.

14

Hyde Park and South Kensington

In spite of their proximity, it would be impossible to cover comprehensively the vast greenery of Hyde Park and the dense cluster of South Kensington museums along its border in a single stroll. Therefore, I have divided this chapter into two very unlike walks. It takes little time to describe, but much time to enjoy the 615 combined acres of Hyde Park and Kensington Gardens. On the other hand, the institutions and museums of South Kensington, though occupying relatively little space, will make intense demands upon your feet—and your sense of wonder. Most walkers will want to combine elements from the two walks, taking a little of this and a little of that, until they have devised an itinerary which suits their touristic taste buds.

Walk One
Hyde Park and Kensington Gardens

Begin: Marble Arch Tube Station
End: High Street Kensington Tube Station

When you leave the Marble Arch tube station, you will be near to Speakers' Corner, and if you're there on a Sunday morning you'll want to take some time to listen to the soapbox orators who preside here on subjects varying from gay rights to religious conversion. You are also relatively near to the spot which served, from 1388 to 1783, as London's primary place of execution. Tyburn Tree, as it was called, was a triangular gallows upon which twenty-one persons could be dispatched at once. Victims were brought in a cart, sometimes accompanied by much ceremony, such as the strewing of flowers by girls in white dresses or the drinking of a farewell mug of ale. Hanging days were public holidays on the theory that the horrible sight would prove a deterrent, though there is not much evidence that it ever did.

Women certainly took their turn dangling from Tyburn Tree. One of the most notable was **Elizabeth Barton** (1506–1534), known as the Holy Maid of Kent. Barton's trances and religious prophecies were very interesting to certain ecclesiastics who felt she could be used to counteract the Protestant movement. She became a nun at Canterbury in 1527, and continued her prophecies, more or less under the direction of Edward Bocking, a monk who trained her in matters of doctrine. But Bocking—or Barton—or God, depending upon whom you believe—went too far. In the king's presence, Barton predicted disaster for Henry VIII should he divorce Catherine of Aragon*, and the king became furious. She confessed when interrogated that she'd been the cat's-paw of the monks and was executed at Tyburn on April 20, 1534.

On November 11, 1615, **Anne Turner*** was executed at Tyburn for her part in the murder of Sir Thomas Overbury. Turner was a dressmaker and costume designer, sometimes employed by Inigo Jones to create costumes for theatrical masques. Her contributions to fashion included the popularization of huge ruffs, kept stiff with yellow starch which she invented. Turner also supplied herbal remedies, and was known as an abortionist and a procuress. When arrested, she stood accused of being a bawd, a sorceress, a witch, a felon, a murderer, and a papist. This last, at least, was probably untrue.

It was **Frances Howard***, Countess of Essex (1594–1632), who probably engineered the murder. Unhappily married to the Earl of Essex, and determined to marry the handsome Scotsman Robert Carr, she apparently engaged in everything from lawsuit to witchcraft to clear away the obstacles to their union. Carr and Howard were both condemned to death for poisoning Overbury, who was Carr's former lover, while Sir Thomas was imprisoned in the Tower. (They feared that Overbury's enmity and his influence over King James I would interfere with their marriage and their fortunes.) But after several years of imprisonment, both were pardoned. Only Turner, who may have provided the fatal poisons, died for her part in the crime.

Both the hangman and Mrs. Turner wore great yellow ruffs at her execution.

In 1683, **Elizabeth Gaunt** (d. 1685), an Anabaptist, was burned to death at Tyburn for harboring a person involved in the unsuccessful Rye House Plot, which aimed to assassinate Charles II. One can have a certain sympathy for women caught up in the political turmoils of their day, but not much for persons like Mrs. **Brownrigg,** who died at Tyburn in 1767 for whipping two female apprentices to death.

As you trek across grassy Hyde Park, reflect upon the fact that boar, wild bull, and deer once roamed where people now recline in their lawn chairs. **Elizabeth I*** (1533–1603) was fond of hunting here and held military reviews on the grounds. The park was opened to the public in the seventeenth century, after which it became quite fashionable, though it was still the site of military camps during emergencies such as the Great Plague and the Jacobite rebellion.

Some writers have set in Hyde Park the famous episode in which **Nell Gwynne*** (1650–1687), mistress to Charles II, was confronted by the mob. According to the story, an angry crowd surrounded and blocked the coach in which she rode, believing it to contain Louise de Kéroüalle, another of Charles' mistresses. During this time of anti-Catholic hysteria and fierce hatred of the French, de Kéroüalle was despised by the people, who called her "the Catholic whore." The people were in an ugly mood, but Nell, as ever, was equal to the emergency. "Good people, desist!" she called out of the coach window. "I am the *Protestant* whore!"

Any open space in London in those times was vulnerable to highwaymen, and Hyde Park was no exception. In 1687 one such criminal was hanged for killing a woman who had swallowed her wedding ring rather than have it taken from her.

It was Queen **Caroline of Anspach*** (1683–1737), the avid landscape architect married to George II, who designed that body of water now known as the Serpentine Lake. Caroline was a big, clever blond with excellent taste in art. George adored her and respected her judgement so much that he consulted her about everything, even his mistresses. In 1729 she was appointed Regent while George was in Hanover and worked closely with Robert Walpole, England's first Prime Minister. Her active role in government gave rise to the jingle:

> *You may strut, dapper George, but 'twill all be in vain;*
> *We know that 'tis Queen Caroline, not you that reign.*

Not quite a hundred years later, the poet Shelley's first wife **Harriet Westbrook** (d. 1816) drowned herself in Caroline's cleverly designed canal, after her husband eloped with Mary Wollstonecraft's* sixteen-year-old daughter, later Mary Shelley*.

Having crossed the water into Kensington Gardens, haunt of Peter Pan (there is a statue of him by the Long Water), make your way to the far end of the park, detouring around the Round Pond. The big brick building before you is Kensington Palace, first occupied by William and **Mary II*** (1662–1694). Mary took an active interest in the reconstruction of the house and especially in the planning of the gardens, which were done in formal Dutch style. Her sister and successor, Queen **Anne***, took a dislike to this style and had the gardens torn up and replaced with something "more English." The orangery to the north of the palace was built for her.

Over a century later, on May 24, 1819, Queen **Victoria*** (1819–

1901) was born in a ground-floor room in Kensington Palace. She was christened Alexandrina Victoria—Alexandrina after Alexander I, tsar of Russia, who was her godfather—and brought up in the palace. Her father died when she was eight, and when she was eleven she became heir presumptive to the throne. There was some expectation of a regency, but William IV hung on, and Victoria had been eighteen for a full twenty-seven days when she became Queen of England.

The statue of Queen Victoria which stands before the palace, executed by her daughter Princess **Louise** (1848–1940), shows her at the time of her coronation. At twenty she married her cousin Albert of Saxe-Coburg, and she is remembered for her devotion to him, but he was her companion for only twenty-two years of her sixty-four-year reign. Victoria and Albert were strong on family life and sexual morality, and their disapproval introduced some restraint—or perhaps a greater sense of privacy—among the licentious elements of the aristocracy. But Victoria's prudery was not always popular, especially during the early part of her reign. When one of her ladies-in-waiting, **Flora Hastings** (1806–1839), suffered a cancerous growth on her liver which caused her to appear pregnant, the queen readily believed the scandalous rumors. Lady Flora was compelled to take a medical examination to prove her virginity, which indeed established her innocence. She died a few months later. But the public faulted the queen for her suspicious nature, and she was hissed on the racecourse at Ascot.

Victoria had a kindly soul but was strictly conservative in her sympathies. She was a strong supporter of charitable schemes and loved loyal working people (but not the agitators who stirred them up). She spoke out strongly on the woman question. "The Queen is most anxious to enlist everyone to join in checking this mad, wicked folly of Women's Rights, with all its attendant horrors, on which her poor feeble sex is bent," she declared royally. "Women would become the most hateful, heartless, and disgusting of human beings were she allowed to unsex herself." Fortunately, not everyone felt compelled to respond to the sovereign's appeal.

Queen Victoria became immensely popular during the latter

part of her reign, both because her sympathies were in agreement with the generally imperialist spirit of the people, and because she had been around so long that few had ever lived under another monarch. In addition to her other state duties, she mothered nine children. (So many of her progeny ended up in the courts of other nations that she has been called the Grandmother of Europe.) It was in childbearing that she made what some might view as a contribution to improving woman's lot: She insisted upon taking chloroform during labor, a practice viewed as cowardly by the menfolk of the day. Her example led many other women to adopt the practice.

When you are done wandering across the green grass, leave Kensington Gardens from the southwest corner and head west along Kensington Road. Turning left on Young Street will bring you into *Kensington Square*, a quiet square with private gardens which has many original houses. The square was first laid out in 1681, but didn't become really fashionable until William and Mary moved into Kensington Palace.

On the west side of the square, in the Queen Anne house at No. 33, you will see a plaque to the actress Mrs. Pat **Campbell*** (1865–1940), who lived here for nineteen years. The house was a gathering place for poets, playwrights, and artists of every kind, including the brilliant young dancer **Isadora Duncan** (1878–1927), who was still in the early stages of her career. Mrs. Pat also counted the portraitist John Singer Sargent among her acquaintances, and coaxed him several times to paint her. Finally he told her flatly: "I cannot paint beautiful women."

But the most interesting of Mrs. Pat's friendships was surely the one with the playwright George Bernard Shaw, with whom she carried on a thirty-year flirtation. She was the original Eliza Doolittle in Shaw's *Pygmalion,* and it was shortly after she first heard him read the play that Shaw (a married man) fell passionately in love with her and began to say so to everyone who would listen. In an early letter, in which he referred to himself in the third person, he warned her: "Oh dont, dont, DONT fall in love with him; but dont grudge him the joy he finds in being in love with you, and writing all sorts of wild but heartfelt exquisite lies—lies, lies, lies, lies to you, his adoredest."

No. 18 was once the home of John Stuart Mill, the English philosopher and economist who as an M.P. presented to the House of Commons the first petition demanding enfranchisement of women. Mill's ideas on women's rights and political economy were much influenced by **Harriet Taylor** (1807–1858), the love of his life. In his autobiography Mill revealed that nearly all his works—including, of course, *On the Subjection of Women* (1869)—were the result of collaborative efforts between the two of them. When Harriet's husband John Taylor died, and she and Mill were at last free to marry (after nineteen years of romantic friendship), Mill made a formal renunciation of the traditional rights of a husband before they took their vows.

No. 14 Kensington Square was the residence of **Alice Stopford Green** (1847–1929), the Irish nationalist and writer. Alice Stopford and John Richard Green, who was also devoted to the Irish cause, met at Oxford. After their marriage they settled into Kensington Square and held salons which were attended by their literary, political, and scholarly friends, including historians. Richard was writing *A Short History of the English People*, a book which Alice finished after his death from tuberculosis six years after they married. In later years she became increasingly militant about the Irish question, and she at last moved to Dublin. After the creation of the Irish Free State she was elected a senator there.

Leave the square by heading north on Derry Street, then turn left into Kensington High Street to find the High Street Kensington tube station.

Walk Two
South Kensington

Begin and End: South Kensington Tube Station

From the South Kensington tube station, follow the signs marked "Subway to Museums" into the pedestrian tunnel, and take the exit for the Victoria and Albert Museum. This will deliver you to the *British Museum (Natural History)*†, which boasts a vast collection of fossils, bones, and carcasses varying from the colossal (dinosaurs and whales) to the miniscule (spiders and mites). Many specimens were collected for the museum by **Mary Kingsley** (1862–1900), an ethnologist and traveller who spent many years in Africa. Kingsley, like most of her generation, was an imperialist, but she was concerned that the development of the African continent should leave the native citizen "a free unsmashed man—not a whitewashed slave or an enemy." She travelled as a trader, in order to have an excuse to study the people, and was as conversant with the art of buying and selling rubber, palm oil, and timber as with the indigenous religions which interested her so much.

The museum's collections also include many fossils gathered by **Mary Anning** (1799–1847), an unschooled woman who is credited with first discovering the remains of the ichthyosaurus at Lyme Regis at the tender age of twelve. She often helped her father gather petrified shells and mollusks from the cliffs near their home; they sold these to summer visitors to help support their family. Anning continued her fossil collecting into her adult life, and numbered the plesiosaurus and pterodactyl among her finds.

When you have had your fill of rocks and bones, move on to the truly overwhelming *Victoria and Albert Museum*† next door. A large structure of terra-cotta brick built to the designs of Aston Webb, the museum was opened in 1909. It is named, of course, for Queen Victoria* and her beloved husband Albert, the Prince Consort. The museum contains some seven miles of well-lighted and well-labelled galleries, and no more diverse collection of artworks can be imagined. In addition to its many national treasures and curiosities, there are collections of Continental, Islamic, Chinese, Japanese, and Indian art. Here you will find paintings, furniture, silver, glass, china, costumes, and textiles. Here centuries of women's art can be viewed in the displays of embroidery, silks, tapestries, lacework, and patchwork quilts. A comprehensive feminist guide to the V&A remains to be written, but by no means confine yourself to the few highlights mentioned below—do your own browsing, for there is much to discover.

The textile collections of the museum include the Oxburgh

hangings, tapestries worked by the illustrious **Mary,** Queen of Scots* (1524–1587), and by her grim "jailer," **Elizabeth Talbot***, better known as Bess of Hardwick. Talbot (1518–1608) had a talent for marrying and a passion for building. She was widowed for the first time at age fifteen, and several times subsequently. Each heartbreak increased her fortune substantially, and with her money she built lavish homes in Derbyshire and elsewhere.

It was officially her final husband, the Earl of Shrewsbury, who was custodian of the Queen of Scots during the sixteen years of her imprisonment at the command of Elizabeth I*. Bess was not completely happy with the attentions and courtesies the earl paid to his prisoner, and the hours the two women spent embroidering together may not have been comfortable ones.

The V&A houses the work of many women flower painters, water colorists, miniaturists, and photographers. Some of these works are light- sensitive and are not on display; however, they can be viewed in the Print Room without prior appointment. Use the extensive catalogs there to locate works by **Mary Moser*** (1744–1819), who is perhaps the most famous of the many women flower painters. Moser was an intimate of the royal family and a founding member of the Royal Academy. The Flemish painter **Levina Teerlinc** (c. 1515–1576) is also represented at the V&A. She was the oldest of miniaturist Simon Benninck's five daughters and was trained by him to illuminate manuscripts. After her marriage to George Teerlinc she came with him to the court of Henry VIII, where she received an annual salary of £40 from Henry as a court painter—more than Holbein was getting. The catalogs in the Print Room will also guide you to oil paintings by the Restoration portraitist **Mary Beale*** (1623–1699), the eighteenth-century Swiss painter **Angelica Kauffmann*** (1741–1807), and by **Vanessa Bell*** (1879–1961) of Bloomsbury fame.

In the European collections you can see a terra-cotta figure by Spanish sculptor **Luisa Roldan** (1656–1704). She was trained in a family workshop in which her sisters and brothers also worked. Together with her husband, Luis de los Arcos, she executed sculptures for the Cadiz cathedral in the 1680s. In 1692 she became the official court sculptor in Madrid, though she was not highly paid.

When you have seen as much of the Victoria and Albert as you can absorb on one visit, you might like to go next door (east) to the *Brompton Oratory* for a few minutes of quiet. The baroque structure was completed in 1884, and will be familiar to lovers of the Clara Batchelor trilogy by **Antonia White** (1899–1980). It is here that Clara knelt in anguished prayer on the eve of her disastrous marriage to Archie Hughes-Follett. The Batchelor trilogy was largely autobiographical; like Clara, White had a brief theatrical career and an unhappy marriage, and was institutionalized for some time after a nervous breakdown. Her earlier novel, *Frost in May*, also autobiographical, told the story of her convent girlhood. It was at the convent that she made her first attempt at writing, making her fictional characters as evil as she could so that their later conversion and repentance would have grand dramatic value. Unhappily, the manuscript was discovered by the nuns before the repentance came about, and White was expelled. This incident had a strong impact on her later writing career, and throughout her life she found creative work stressful and difficult.

In addition to writing fiction, White worked as a translator— her translations of Colette's works are particularly well known—and as a free-lance journalist, theater critic, and fashion editor.

Retrace your steps to Exhibition Road and turn right (north), following it past its junctions with Imperial College and Prince Consort roads. Before turning left into Kensington Gore, you'll see the red brick buildings of the *Royal Geographic Society* on your left. The Society was founded in 1830 and combined several previous groups, such as the Travellers Club and the African Society. But these bold explorers were not yet ready for the adventure of having a woman as one of their number.

It was **Isabella Bishop** (1831–1904) who was the first female to be elected a fellow of the Society. Bishop began travelling at age forty, upon the recommendation of a doctor who said a change of scene would improve her health. She travelled alone through the Rocky Mountains, Japan, India, the Kashmir, Tibet, and Korea, working as a cowgirl, a cook, and a missionary along the way. She founded hospitals in India and Tibet, and recorded her journeys through her writings and photographs. When she married she said that she'd love to visit New Guinea on her honeymoon, but that it was hardly the kind of place you could take a man. She was sixty-eight when she explored Morocco and the Atlas Mountains.

Another interesting traveller was **Kate Marsden** (1859–1931), a trained nurse who worked in a leper colony in Siberia in the 1890s. She was elected a fellow of the Society in 1892, but in 1894 she was refused a ticket to the annual dinner on the grounds that she would be the only woman among nearly two hundred men—all of them smoking.

Turn left into Kensington Gore and you will find yourself before the famous *Albert Hall,* a great oval building of brick under a glass and iron dome. The Hall was built on the site of Gore House, once the home of **Marguerite,** Countess of Blessington (1789–1849). An Irishwoman of great beauty, shrewd mind, extravagant tastes, and strong will, she abandoned two different husbands before she discovered a man to her liking. She and the Count D'Orsay—her stepdaughter's husband— lived openly together in London, while Marguerite wrote light novels and sketches in an increasingly futile attempt to keep the wolf from their door. In her more prosperous days, the countess was a great patron of the arts, and Thackeray and Dickens were among the visitors who came to her salons at Gore House.

Since its construction, the Albert Hall has been used for such diverse events as concerts, balls, festivals, boxing matches, and, yes, suffragette rallies.

The first suffragette presence at the Hall came at a great meeting on December 21, 1905, at which the new Prime Minister, Sir Henry Campbell-Bannerman, spoke. At the conclusion of his speech the suffragette **Annie Kenney*** (1879–1953) flourished a banner, calling out: "Will the Liberal government give women the vote?" At the same moment, **Theresa Billington-Greig*** (1877–1964) from a seat just above the platform, unfurled an immense banner bearing the question: "Will the Liberal government give justice to working women?" The audience gasped,

Dame Ethel Smythe

people cried out, and the women were hastily evicted from the Hall.

Just over two years later, the suffragettes were back, but this time they had the Hall to themselves. On March 19, 1908, the largest indoor rally in support of women's suffrage that had ever been held took place here. The women present believed **Emmeline Pankhurst*** (1858–1928) to be still serving a prison sentence for militant acts, and were greatly moved by her empty chair upon the stage as they listened to **Christabel Pankhurst*** (1880–1958) hold forth. Midway through the meeting, however, the crowd was electrified by the arrival of Emmeline, recently released.

That was the first of many meetings the suffragettes held in Albert Hall, meetings which often ended in thousands of women marching to Parliament Square or Downing Street. Emmeline Pankhurst and **Emmeline Pethick-Lawrence*** (1867–1954) dominated the platform, until the day that the Women's Social and Political Union suffered a split. On that occasion, Emmeline Pankhurst addressed the women before her gravely, saying,

> *Whenever I stand upon this platform in the Albert Hall I can never feel that I am speaking to an ordinary political meeting. It seems to me rather that I am assisting at a review, and tonight I feel more than ever that we are reviewing our forces. . . . In an army you need unity of purpose. In an army you also need unity of policy. . . .*

She went on to explain that Mrs. Pethick-Lawrence and her husband would henceforth be working in their own way for women's suffrage, and not as part of the WSPU. It may have been partly Emmeline's sense of herself as a general at the head of an army that made the Pethick-Lawrences agree at last to a separation of forces.

Dame **Ethel Mary Smythe** (1858–1944) may very well have been present at some of these suffragette rallies, as she was an active supporter of the cause. But she was no newcomer to Albert Hall. In 1893, her Mass in D was performed there, bringing her compositions the recognition in England which they had already been accorded in Germany. Smythe's early works were for orchestral and chamber music; later she wrote operas and large choral works. In 1916 she wrote a comic opera with a feminist viewpoint called *The Boatswain's Mate*. She was also the composer of a suffragette anthem called "March of the Women," and on one occasion, when imprisoned in Holloway for militant action, she led the other suffragettes in the singing of the stirring song, conducting with her toothbrush.

More recently, Albert Hall has hosted conductor-composer **Avril Coleridge-Taylor** (b. 1903), daughter of the composer Samuel Coleridge-Taylor. This gifted musician made her debut as a composer at age thirteen, in London. Sixteen years later she made her debut as a conductor, in Eastbourne. Between 1936 and 1960 she was a guest conductor for the BBC Symphony Orchestra, and between 1943 and 1950 she conducted the Coleridge-Taylor Symphony Orchestra.

Circle around to the back of the Albert Hall and walk through the plaza to the *Royal College of Music*, which is at the west end of Prince Consort Road. **Jenny Lind*** (1820–1887) was one of the first instructors at the College. As there was as yet no facility appropriate for the lessons, Lind's students were taught in her own spacious drawing room. The singer was sixty-three by this time and had been retired from singing for many years, although she not infrequently broke her retirement in order to give benefit concerts. Even at the height of her career, benefit concerts seemed to be Lind's greatest interest, for causes ranging from the improvement of nursing (under Florence Nightingale*) to social work done at the Victoria docks. But her very favorite cause was always the education and training of singers and musicians, especially in her native Sweden. Lind herself had been able to receive her training only through such aid, and she always felt very grateful.

One of Lind's students was the mulatto musician **Amanda Ira Aldridge** (b. 1866), who won a singing scholarship to the College in 1883. She later taught and composed under the name Montagu Ring. Her works included love songs, sambas, and light orchestral pieces, including one called "Three African Dances." Her students included Marian Anderson and Paul Robeson.

The famous contralto **Clara Butt*** (1873–1937) studied here in 1890. She went on to win renown as a concert artist and did many charity concerts during World War I.

Turn right into Prince Consort Road and left into Queen's Gate, and you will shortly come to an entrance to the South Kensington tube station.

15

Chelsea

Begin and End: Sloane Square Tube Station

When Sir Thomas More first established his Chelsea estate in the early sixteenth century, the area was merely a quiet riverside village difficult of access—except by water. In its many incarnations Chelsea has known the nobility in their manor houses, the hurly-burly of the wharf, streets filled with poverty and vice, and innumerable writers, actors, and artists. In the sixties it became the home of the miniskirt, popularized, to the sorrow of many feminists, by the radical fashion innovator, **Mary Quant** (b. 1934). More lately still it has been the scene of a colorful punk subculture. But the Chelsea of today has one thing in common with More's Chelsea; there is still a difficulty with transportation. The Sloane Square station is the only underground stop in the area, and though you can spare your feet a bit by taking busses, be forewarned that the walk which follows is one of the longer sojourns included in this book.

As you leave the *Sloane Square* tube station, you will be very near the Royal Court Theatre, located on the east side of the square. Here, in 1955, the black actress **Connie Smith** (1877–1970) played Tituba in a production of Arthur Miller's *The Crucible*, at the age of seventy-eight. Smith first left her native New York for Europe at age seventeen, performing in a show titled *The South Before the War and After*. For many years she and her husband, Augustus Smith, were a popular song and dance act, and it was only in her later years that she turned to straight theater.

Begin your tour of Chelsea by walking southwest on King's Road, the liveliest of Chelsea streets, which will take you past many bright and trendy boutiques. (If you prefer, you can take a bus as far as Beaufort Street, about a half mile.) From King's Road turn left into *Beaufort Street*, walking toward the river. You are now near, or perhaps on, the site of Sir Thomas More's estate. He lived here in the early 1600s with his large family, including his second wife Dame **Alice More*** (d. 1571). They were apparently fond companions, sharing a love of animals and music. Alice kept several small dogs of her own (in addition to her husband's monkeys, rabbits, foxes, and ferrets), and played the lute and virginals. She was known to have a shrewish tongue, and when she visited her husband in the Tower she upbraided him for risking his life and property for something so ephemeral as a principle. In addition to missing his presence at their fireside, she was finding it somewhat of a strain to come up with the fifteen shillings a week required for her husband's board in the Tower and finally had to sell some of her clothes to raise the money. After More's execution she was granted a small allowance by the king and was turned out of her home.

At the end of Beaufort Street, on the right-hand side as you face the Thames, is No. 91 *Cheyne Walk* (which actually faces Beaufort). This was once the home of the essayist **Margaret Fairless Barber** (1869–1901), who wrote under the name of Michael Fairless. Born in Yorkshire, she came to work as a nurse in a London slum, where she was known as the "Fighting Sister," but had to give up the work due to ill health. For a time she lived a reclusive life in a roadside cottage where she dispensed charity to the tramps who came to her door, and later she came to Chelsea. Her most famous work, *The Roadmender*, is a devotional work written during the last two years of her life, the final chapter of which was dictated literally on her deathbed. She died at age thirty-two. All her works were posthumously published.

Turn right into Cheyne Walk for a look at No. 93, which bears a plaque (situated between two windows on an upper story) to the novelist **Elizabeth Gaskell***, nee Stevenson (1810–1865), who was born here. Her mother survived her birth only a month, and Elizabeth was sent to an aunt in the country town that became the model for *Cranford* (1853), a gently ironic tale of village life. In 1832 she married William Gaskell, a Unitarian minister, and went with him to Manchester, where she was able to observe some of the ignoble effects of the industrial revolution. She was the mother of five children and began writing only after the death of a baby son from scarlet fever. Her novel *Ruth* (1853) was controversial because it included a sympathetic portrait of a prostitute; in *North and South* (1855) she explored the lives of working people. She also wrote a classic biography of Charlotte Brontë* (1857).

In the early part of the twentieth century the painter Dame **Ethel Walker** (1861–1951) also lived in Cheyne Walk, in a house situated a little bit further west, beyond the Chelsea Wharf. In later life she grew somewhat reclusive and kept company chiefly with her many cats, whom she fed on steak and milk. At this time, too, she was crippled with arthritis and had difficulty holding a brush, but she continued to paint.

Though Walker was interested in art from her girlhood, she received no formal training until she was thirty years old. She made up for lost time by becoming one of the leading members of the New English Art Club around the turn of the century (along with Philip Steer, who also lived in Chelsea). She was later influenced by the impressionists, and it is upon her mature work that her reputation rests. Her work is represented in the collection at the Tate Gallery.

Reverse your direction and proceed east on Cheyne Walk, and you will soon see Crosby Hall upon your left. This sixteenth-century building is the only surviving part of a large manor which originally stood in Bishopsgate. It was transferred to Chelsea

stone by stone in 1910. In this building **Catherine of Aragon***
(1485–1536) was feasted by the Lord Mayor of London upon her
arrival in England, and in 1839 **Elizabeth Fry*** (1780–1845) used
it to hold a bazaar "in aid of Female Prisoners and Convicts." It
is now part of the International Hostel of the British Federation
of University Women.

Just before you reach Old Church Street you'll come to a brick-
walled plot of grass known as Roper Gardens, constructed in
1964 on the site of buildings destroyed during the war. The
gardens are a reminder of **Margaret Roper*** (1505–1544), the
English scholar who was Sir Thomas More's daughter. Roper
studied Greek, Latin, philosophy, astronomy, mathematics, and
music, and translated Erasmus's *Treatise on the Lord's Prayer*.
When she married William Roper in 1521, the site which the
garden now occupies was part of her dower property.

Across *Old Church Street* is Chelsea Old Church, much restored after severe damage suffered during World War II, but still
of ancient lineage. A large, seated statue of Thomas More can be
seen outside, and inside dozens of interesting women from
Chelsea's past are commemorated. This wealth of history is due
to the presence of the embroidered kneelers there, which were
begun in the early fifties as the parish sought to restore a sense
of its history in the wake of the terrible destruction suffered from
the war. The kneelers, some of which are quite striking, commemorate hundreds of former parishioners, including a large
number of women. Allow yourself some time to move up and
down the aisles, studying the names, quotations, and symbols
chosen to represent the women of Chelsea. Don't miss the
kneeler dedicated to **Anne Chamberlayne Spragg** (1667–1691).
Anne, of an adventurous disposition, turned down her early
chances of marriage. Dressed and armed as a man, she joined her
brother Peregrine, a naval officer, on his ship and fought the
French under his command in a battle off Beachy Head in June
of 1690. She survived the dangers of war and returned to Chelsea to marry—only to lose her life in childbirth the following
year.

Another kneeler commemorates the Canadian **Yvonne Green**
(1911–1941), one of five fire wardens who died on the night of

April 16, 1941, when the church was badly damaged by a German bomb.

Chelsea Old Church commemorates women in stone as well as in textiles. The More Monument, on the south side of the sanctuary, includes a Latin inscription which praises Dame **Alice More***, in particular her virtue as a stepmother. The text was written by her husband, Sir Thomas More. In a southeast corner of the church is a wall tablet in memory of four women of Chelsea who were "distinguished by their learning and piety." These include the early feminist and pamphleteer **Mary Astell*** and the botanical artist **Elizabeth Blackwell***, both of whom worshipped here and were buried in the churchyard.

The north wall of the church is dominated by the memorial to Lady **Jane Cheyne** (1620–1669), its benefactor. Jane was daughter to the Royalist William Cavendish, first Duke of Newcastle, and after his flight to Holland she and her sisters held their estate for several days against the Cromwellian forces. She sold all her jewels to raise money for her father in his exile, but after the Restoration her family regained its wealth, and Jane was able to extend her generosity beyond the family, which she did by giving substantial sums to aid in the rebuilding of the church. She was much loved, and much mourned by her husband and the community when she died. The unusual monument, which was constructed in Italy from a portrait and shipped to England, was said to be an amazing likeness.

To continue up Cheyne Walk you must keep to the left, away from the Chelsea Embankment. When you come to *Cheyne Row* turn left, and you will soon see No. 10, an old brick house with brick archways which was once the home of **Margaret Damer Dawson** (1875–1920). Dawson is best known for founding the Women Police Volunteers, which she did in 1914. The organization trained hundreds of women to do preventive patrolling of London, assisting with refugee settlement, rescue work during air raids, and munitions work. The women were hindered in their work by having no power of arrest. In 1918, the Metropolitan Police sued Dawson for impersonating a police officer, and in 1920 she was convicted and given a token fine. Dawson's activities also included animal welfare work.

At No. 24 Cheyne Row is Carlyle's House† (steps), where the famous Victorian historian lived with his wife, **Jane Welsh Carlyle*** (1801–1866). The house, which is open to the public, is a little on the dank side, but it is much as it was when the Carlyles lived there. Most of the furnishings and books were theirs, and the walls are filled with prints, engravings, and portraits of the Carlyles and their friends. Jane was playful, satiric, and intelligent, and always meant to do something with her life. As a child she wanted to learn Latin, as boys did. In aid of this she once hid beneath a table in the drawing room, and startled her parents by reciting a few phrases of Latin learned from a local tutor, afterwards saying: "I want to learn Latin; please let me be a boy." Her father, who doted on her, surrendered, but the Latin lessons were evidently insufficient to launch her into a literary career. When she and Carlyle began corresponding, he encouraged her in her literary aspirations—until she at last agreed to marry him. Then he assumed that she would be fully occupied in taking care of him.

In Chelsea, Jane found that she was indeed fully occupied in nurturing her husband's genius, though she was not precisely a devoted wife—the two were famous for their quarrels. She was, however, an efficient household manager, and in addition to overseeing the shopping, cleaning, meal preparation, and entertaining, she had tasks such as trying to keep the neighbor's roosters from annoying Carlyle with their crowing, and paying all the bills—including the income taxes, with which Victorian wives were not generally burdened. She found in her life much that was suitable for her comic, ironic letters and monologues, and her lively wit won her a following of her own among the literary lights of Chelsea. In the library of the house—where you will see a screen that she decorated—Jane received her friends: Dickens, Tennyson, Browning, and Darwin, among others. It was from her chair before the fireplace in the sitting room that she jumped up to greet Leigh Hunt when he came to see her after having been ill, inspiring his wonderful rondeau, *Jenny Kissed Me*.

Though the Queen Anne houses on Cheyne Row have not changed much since the days the Carlyles lived there, you will not have to cope, as Jane did, with the cries of cocks, the music of organ grinders, the rattle of carts and handbarrows over cobblestones, or a wandering Punch & Judy show.

Retrace your steps to *Cheyne Walk* and continue east. While passing the Shrewsbury House flats you might reflect that they are built upon the site of old Shrewsbury House, originally built in 1519 for the fourth Earl of Shrewsbury. A couple of generations later George, sixth Earl of Shrewsbury, lived there with his wife, Bess of Hardwick, also known as **Elizabeth Talbot*** (1518–1608). Bess and the earl didn't get along very well, and the tension was increased by the fact that **Mary,** Queen of Scots* (1524–1587), was their houseguest/prisoner. Bess was jealous of the great attention and devotion that the earl gave to the prisoner, and finally accused the two of being lovers. This prompted an investigation, and Bess had to change her tune, declaring upon her knees at a public inquiry that her accusation had been untrue. Finally, in 1583, Bess couldn't take it anymore. She left her husband and moved to the countryside, where she consoled herself by building magnificent castles.

Cheyne Walk is shortly intersected by *Oakley Street*, where Lady **Speranza Wilde** (1821–1896) once lived in a house which is now gone. Wilde was an Irish patriot who in her youth wrote ardent political articles and poems. When she came to Chelsea she was long widowed, a large woman given to heavy makeup, clanking jewelry, eccentricity in dress, and drama in speech. She gave brilliant afternoon parties, which were often attended by her more famous son Oscar, who lived not far off in Tite Street. In April of 1895 Oscar was arrested at the nearby Cadogan Hotel on a charge of sodomy. He was eventually sentenced to two years hard labor. Between the two trials he stayed for a time with his mother in Oakley Street.

Continue east on Cheyne Walk, and shortly after passing Oakley Street you'll see a plaque marking the site where Henry VIII's Manor House once stood. The palace was intended for his bride **Jane Seymour,** whom he married secretly at Chelsea Old Church. Seymour was a queen who could live with Henry's ideas about religious independence; she herself carried on extensive correspondence with religious reformers in Europe—in

Latin, of course. Alas, she died a few days after giving him the male heir he so desired, and the Manor was turned instead into a nursery for their son Edward—and, incidentally, for **Elizabeth I*** (1533–1603), his daughter by Anne Boleyn*. Special attention was paid to the magnificent gardens, for the maintenance of which twenty-nine gardeners and six women weeders were employed.

Later, when the king married his sixth and final wife, **Katherine Parr** (1512–1548), he gave her the Manor at Chelsea as part of her jointure. A calm and tactful woman, Parr got along with Henry rather better than most people did. She was a good stepmother to his children, and a good nurse to Henry in his final illness. She was another queen who was interested in theology; she wrote religious poetry and edited a book of *Prayers and Meditations*.

On December 3, 1880, the literary lioness **George Eliot*** (1819–1880) moved with her new husband, John Cross, into No. 4 Cheyne Walk, which you'll find just before Cheyne Walk ends at Royal Hospital Road. The house, which is fronted with fine wrought iron work, was built in 1716. Eliot hoped to recover her health in Chelsea's mild air, but died only nineteen days after her arrival.

Eliot was an intellectual and a freethinker. She wrote about rationalism and theology, studied the classics, did translations from German, and knew every important writer and thinker in England. But her great contribution to literature rests upon her magnificent novels, which employ a deep, sensitive realism in their examination of the human soul. Her masterwork, *Middlemarch*, has been called by some the greatest novel in the English language.

At the end of Cheyne Walk, veer left into *Royal Hospital Road*, once known as Paradise Row. An early resident of the Row was the feminist **Mary Astell*** (1666–1731). Astell was the daughter of a Newcastle merchant, but she came to Chelsea at age twenty and lived there almost fifty years. In 1694 she published a work entitled: *A Serious Proposal to the Ladies, for the Advancement of Their Time and Greatest Interest*, which argued that education for women would aid their virtue and combat their vices. "When a poor young lady is taught to value herself on nothing but her clothes . . . who can blame her if she lay out her industry and money on such accomplishments, and sometimes extends it farther than her misinformer desires she should?" she wrote. Astell proposed a scheme whereby interested women would live a cloistered, scholastic life. The suggestion met with much interest, controversy, and ridicule, but was eventually quashed by Bishop Burnett.

Another work by Astell, titled *Some Reflections Upon Marriage Occasioned by the Duke and Duchess of Mazarin's Case*, was inspired by her neighbor in Paradise Row, **Hortense,** Duchesse de Mazarin. In her youth in France, Hortense was married by her uncle, a cardinal, to the Duc de la Meilleraye, who was known to be mad as a hatter. Her husband shut her in a convent for awhile, where she amused herself playing pranks on the nuns, but eventually she fled France, disguised as a boy and pursued all the while by the duke. Upon her arrival in England she became Charles II's mistress, and it was not until after his death that she came to live in Paradise Row with her cats, dogs, monkeys, parrots, and starlings. Though she was much in debt, she gave exciting parties with the best musicians available. (She is said by some to have introduced Italian opera to England.) After her death the mad duke paid her debts and was rewarded with her corpse; he had it embalmed and carried it with him wherever he went.

On your right you will find the Chelsea Physic Garden, which has been here since 1673. The entrance is in *Swan Walk*. It was here that **Elizabeth Blackwell*** (1689–1758), who lived in Swan Walk, made careful drawings of the flowers and fruits used by apothecaries for medicinal purposes. Daughter of an Aberdeen merchant, Elizabeth eloped with Alexander Blackwell and came with him to London. When her husband was imprisoned for setting up as a printer without having served an apprenticeship, she began to earn the family's living doing drawings and copper engravings for physicians. Her work *A Curious Herbal containing Five Hundred Cuts of the most Useful Plants which are now used in the Practice of Physick* was a multivolume effort which appeared in the 1730s. Each plate showed the flower, fruit, seed, and sometimes the root of the plant. With her earnings, Blackwell redeemed her husband from prison, though later he came to a bad end in Sweden where his rash speeches led to his being executed for conspiracy against the crown.

From the greenery of Swan Walk turn left into Dilke Street and you will shortly pass the entrance to *Paradise Walk,* on your left. It was probably at the south end of the walk, facing the Thames, that Turret House once stood. (Dilke Street did not yet exist.) **Sarah Banks** (d. 1804) came to live there in 1761, after the death of her husband. Mother of the famous botanist Sir Joseph Banks, Sarah was the one who encouraged him to follow his heart in his peculiar studies at the nearby physic garden, rather than taking up the family career of politics. She was said to be a strong woman, "void of all imaginary fear." She was also a religious woman, and upon moving to Chelsea she was much influenced by the Moravians, who were pacifists and fierce opponents of slavery.

One evening Mrs. Banks heard terrible screams coming from the water, and ran out to see what had occurred. It turned out that a man named Robert Stapylton had hired some ruffians to kidnap Thomas Lewis, who had formerly been his slave. Her servants arrived too late to prevent Lewis from being carried away by boat, but Banks sent for the famous abolitionist lawyer, Granville Sharp, and told him that she would pay all expenses involved in bringing Stapylton and his men to justice. Sharp secured the release of Thomas and won a verdict of guilty against Stapylton, but the justice in the case refused to give sentence.

Sir Joseph's sister **Sophie Banks** (d. 1818), who never married, was an eccentric Chelsea intellectual of masculine appearance. She had enormous pockets especially made in her skirts, so that she could stuff them with books of all sizes.

Paradise Walk today is a changing mixture of modern flats and charming cottages with bright shutters and flower boxes, but in Victorian times the street was a notorious slum, frequented by pickpockets and prostitutes.

Return to Dilke Street, and turn left and then right (on Tite Street, where Oscar Wilde once lived) to reach the *Chelsea Em-*

bankment. Turn left and continue east, and you will pass before the Chelsea Royal Hospital, founded by Charles II for retired army veterans and used for the same purpose today. (You may see some of the Chelsea Pensioners strolling about the neighborhood in their bright red coats.) The building, by Sir Christopher Wren, has not been greatly altered over the centuries, though there were a few eighteenth-century additions. The infirmary, to the west of the hospital, stands on the site of a home once occupied by the statesman Sir Robert Walpole, and Queen **Caroline of Anspach*** (1683–1737) came there to consult with him. When he first met her Walpole took a dislike to Caroline and referred to the portly princess as a "fat bitch." But after she became queen he changed his mind about her, and they governed brilliantly together while George II was in Hanover.

To the east of the hospital are Ranelagh Gardens, which in the eighteenth century were popular and respectable pleasure gardens offering music (Mozart himself once performed here), booths for drinking tea or wine and others for gentlemen who wished to smoke, an ornamental lake, a Chinese pavilion, and fireworks. In **Fanny Burney's*** (1752–1840) novel *Evelina,* the title character says of Ranelagh: "It is a charming place, and the brilliancy of the lights, on my first entrance, made me almost think I was in some inchanted [sic] castle, or fairy palace, for all looked like magic to me."

At the corner of the Chelsea Embankment and *Chelsea Bridge Road* you'll find the buildings of Lister Hospital, in redbrick and yellow stone. It was in 1910 that the biochemist **Ida Smedley-MacLean** (1877–1944) first came to do research at the Lister Institute of Preventive Medicine. She remained associated with the Institute for the remainder of her life, becoming a staff member in 1932. Smedley-MacLean did significant work on fat metabolism and fat synthesis. In addition to her scientific contribution, she was an active member of the British Federation of University Women, which supported women's suffrage and educational and research opportunities for women. Her special interest was the opening of learned societies to women, and in 1904—the same year that Madame Marie Curie was made an honorary member of the Chemical Society—she presented a petition to the Council of the Society, signed by nineteen women chemists, requesting that women be granted membership. Four years later the Council created a sort of partial membership for women, but only a few took advantage of this largess; most preferred to hope for better things. When, in 1920, women were finally admitted to full membership, Ida Smedley-MacLean was the first woman formally received.

In the late 1920s, **Margaret Boas** did research at the Lister Institute which led to the identification of the B complex vitamin Biotin.

To return to Sloane Square turn left into Chelsea Bridge Road and follow it north until (after becoming Lower Sloane Street) it leads you to the square. Or, if your feet are tired, you can catch a #137 bus which will deliver you to the tube station.

Appendix: Hours and Access

British Museum
Great Russell Street
London WC1 3DG
01-636 1555

Hours: Monday to Saturday, 10–5; Sunday, 2:30–6. Closed during the Christmas period (Christmas Eve, Christmas Day, and Boxing Day), New Year's Day, Good Friday, and the first Monday in May.

Access: Many, though not all, galleries are accessible to those in wheelchairs. Elevator is at the left-hand side of the steps up to the main entrance; press button to call a warder. Two unisex lavatories on ground floor for those in wheelchairs. Further information available from the Education Service, British Museum, London WC1B 3DG.

Admission: Free

British Museum (Natural History)
Cromwell Road
London SW7
01-589 6323

Hours: Monday to Saturday, 10–6; Sunday, 1–6.

Access: The museum is accessible to those in wheelchairs, but prior notification is necessary to operate the lifts (elevators) behind the museum.

Admission: £2.60 for adults; £1.25 for children.

Carlyle's House
24 Cheyne Row
London SW3 5HL
01-352 7087

Hours: April to October, Wednesday to Sunday, and Bank Holiday Mondays, 11–5. Last admission, 4:30. Closed Good Friday.

Access: Carlyle's House is not accessible to those in wheelchairs.

Admission: £1.60

Fawcett Library
City of London Polytechnic
Calcutta House
Old Castle Street
London E1 7NT
01-283 1030 Ext. 570

Hours: During term: Monday, 11–8:30; Wednesday to Friday, 10–5. During vacation: Monday, Wednesday, and Friday, 10–5. Closed public holidays, Tuesdays, and weekends throughout the year, from Maundy Thursday to the Tuesday after Easter, and from December 24 to January 1. Occasional lunchtime closures during vacation.

Access: The library is accessible to those in wheelchairs, but prior notification is necessary so that the street door near the elevator, which is ordinarily kept locked, can be opened.

Admission: The fee for day use is £2.00, or £1.00 for students and unemployed; no borrowing privileges granted. Those who want to do research over a longer period of time can subscribe to the library for £10.00 (£5.00 for full-time students or unemployed); this includes borrowing privileges.

Gray's Inn
Treasury Office
5 South Square
London WC1
01-405 8164

Hours: You can stroll through the Inn any time during the daylight hours, Monday to Friday. Gardens open 12–2:30. Ask at the library about touring the interiors of the buildings.

Access: Interiors of some of the buildings not accessible to those in wheelchairs.

Admission: Free (except for tours)

Guildhall
Gresham Street
P.O. Box 270
London EC2P 2EJ
01-260 1456 or 01-606 3030

Hours: Seven days a week, 10–5 May to September; Monday to Saturday, 10–5 October to April.

Access: Wheelchairs must be lifted up three steps to enter the banqueting hall. Most other parts of the Guildhall are not accessible.

Admission: Free

Inner Temple
Treasurer's Office
Inner Temple
London EC4Y 7HL
01-353 8462

Hours: The Fleet Street gate giving onto the grounds is open Monday to Saturday, 8–8. The Embankment Gate can be used to gain access to the grounds at other hours. The Inn itself is open only to groups who have made prior written arrangement for tours. The Temple Church is open seven days a week from 10–4, except when services, weddings, choir practices, and special events are in progress. It is generally closed during August and September.

Access: The church has one shallow step.

Admission: Free

Jewish Museum
Woburn House
Tavistock Square
London WC1H 0EP
01-388 4525

Hours: Tuesday to Thursday (and Friday during the summer), 10–4; Sunday (and Friday during the winter), 10–12:45 P.M. Closed Mondays, Saturdays, and Jewish holidays.

Access: Accessible to those in wheelchairs.

Admission: Free, but a 50p. donation is encouraged.

Lincoln's Inn
Chief Porter
11a New Square
London WC2
01- 405 6360

Hours: You can stroll around the buildings anytime during the daylight hours Monday to Friday. Gardens open 12–2:30 P.M. Guided tours of the buildings available 9:30–11:30, March–September, £2, ask at porter's lodge. Closed Saturdays and Sundays.

Access: Most of the buildings are not accessible to those in wheelchairs.

Admission: Free (except for tours)

Madame Tussaud's Waxworks
Marylebone Road
London NW1 5LR
01-935 6861

Hours: In summer, Monday to Sunday, 9–6:30, last admission at 5:30. In winter, 9:30–6:30, last admission at 5:30.

Access: All parts of the museum are accessible to those in wheelchairs.

Admission: £4.95

Middle Temple
Under Treasurer
Treasury Office
Middle Temple
2 Plowden Buildings
Middle Temple Lane
London EC4Y 9AT
01-353 4355

Hours: The Fleet Street gate giving onto the grounds is open Monday to Saturday, 8–8. The Embankment Gate can be used to gain access to the grounds at other hours. The Middle Temple Hall is open Monday to Friday, 10–11:30 A.M. and 3–4 P.M.; it is closed in August. The Temple Church is open seven days a week from 10–4, except when services, weddings, choir practices, and special events are in progress. It is generally closed during

August and September.

Access: The church has one shallow step. The Middle Temple Hall is reached by a shallow flight of steps; those in wheelchairs can be lifted if prior arrangement is made with the porters.

Admission: Free

The Monument
Monument Street
London EC3

Hours: Summer (March 31 to September 30): Monday to Friday, 9–6, Saturday and Sunday, 2–6. Winter (October 1 to March 30): Monday to Saturday, 9–4, closed Sundays. Last admission twenty minutes before closing.

Access: Not accessible to those in wheelchairs.

Admission: 50p.

Museum of London
London Wall
London EC2Y 5HN
01-600 3699

Hours: Tuesday to Saturday, 10–6, last admission 5:30. Closed every Monday. Open Bank Holidays.

Access: All parts of the museum are accessible by wheelchair, and a tape guide and braille sheets are available for partially sighted and blind visitors. There are lavatories for the disabled.

Admission: Free

National Gallery
Trafalgar Square
London WC2N 5DN
01-839 3321

Hours: Monday to Saturday, 10–6, Sunday, 2–6. In August and September, the Wednesday hours are from 10–8.

Access: Most galleries are accessible to those in wheelchairs. Enter by the east entrance, to the right of the Trafalgar Square entrance.

Admission: Free

National Portrait Gallery
St. Martin's Place
London WC2H 0HE
01-930 1552

Hours: Monday to Friday, 10–5, Saturday, 10–6, and Sunday, 2–6. Closed New Year's Day, Good Friday, May Day Bank Holiday, Christmas Eve, Christmas Day, and Boxing Day.

Access: Those in wheelchairs must be carried down one flight of stairs from the lobby to the elevator, which gives access to all galleries.

Admission: Free

Natural History Museum.
See British Museum (Natural History)

Royal Academy of Arts
Burlington House, Piccadilly
London W1
01-439 4996/4997

Hours: Monday to Sunday, 10–6.

Access: All public areas except the restaurant are accessible to those in wheelchairs. To book wheelchairs in advance, call 01-437 7438.

Admission: Varies according to the exhibits, but there is no charge to view the ceiling paintings in the lobby.

St. Paul's Cathedral
The Chapter House
St. Paul's Churchyard
London EC4M 8AD
01-248 4619

Hours: 10–4:15, Monday to Friday and from 11–4:15, Saturday. The crypt and treasury are not open on Sundays, though visitors may stroll around the main part of the cathedral between services. There may be occasional unannounced closings due to special services.

Access: The main part of the cathedral and the crypt are wheelchair accessible, but you will need to contact a verger in order to be taken down to the crypt in the elevator. There is a lavatory accessible to those in wheelchairs in the crypt.

Admission: The main part of the cathedral is free; entrance to crypt and treasury, £1.10; entrance to Whispering Gallery, £2.00.

Tate Gallery
Millbank
London SW1P 4RG
01-821 7128

Hours: Monday to Saturday, 10–5:50, Sunday, 2–5:50. Closed New Year's Day, Good Friday, May Day Holiday, Christmas Eve, and Boxing Day.

Access: The Tate Gallery is accessible to those in wheelchairs through the elevator at the Atterbury Street entrance, but the staff must be notified in advance (01-821 1313 ext. 259 or 260). For reasons of safety no more than six wheelchairs at a time are allowed in the Gallery. Coffee Shop and Restaurant are accessible to those in wheelchairs. There is an induction loop system in the lecture room, and one lecture per month is interpreted for the hearing-impaired.

Admission: Free

Tower of London
Tower Hill
London, EC3
01-709 0765

Hours: March to October, Monday to Saturday, 9:30–5; Sunday, 2–5. November to February, Monday to Saturday, 9:30–4, closed Sunday.

Access: Spiral staircases in the Tower, steps at the jewel house, and cobblestoned grounds make the Tower of London not very accessible to those in wheelchairs. However, there are wheelchair-accessible lavatories.

Admission: Adults, £4.80; senior citizens and students, £3; handicapped visitors, £3; free admission for those accompanying people in wheelchairs.

Victoria and Albert Museum
Cromwell Road
London SW7 2RL
01-938 8500

Hours: Monday to Saturday, 10–5:50; Sunday, 2:30–5:50. There may be unannounced closures of specific galleries due to shortages of staff.

Access: Most galleries are accessible to those in wheelchairs. Contact the chief warder (01-938 8540) for assistance.

Admission: Free, but a £2 donation is suggested.

Westminster Abbey
20 Dean's Yard
London SW1P 3PA
01-222 5152
Nave and Cloisters

Hours: Monday to Saturday except Wednesday, 8–6; Wednesday, 8–7:45; Sunday, between services only.

Access: Accessible to those in wheelchairs.

Admission: Free.

Royal Chapels, Poet's Corner, Choir and Statesmen's Aisle

Hours: Monday to Friday, 9–4:45, last admission 4 p.m.; Saturdays, 9–2:45, last admission 2 p.m. and 3:45 to 5:45, last admission 5 p.m.

Access: The Henry VII Chapel and Confessor's Chapel are not accessible to those in wheelchairs, but the choir aisles, transepts (including Poet's Corner), and ambulatory are.

Admission: £2.20, students £1.10.

Pyx Chamber

Hours: Monday to Saturday, 10:30–4.

Access: Accessible to those in wheelchairs.

Admission: £1.60, students 80p (includes entrance to the Chapter House and museum)

Selected Bibliography

Adler, Michael. *Jews of Medieval England*. London: Jewish Historical Society of England, 1939.

Bachmann, Donna G. and Sherry Piland. *Women Artists: An Historical, Contemporary and Feminist Bibliography*. Metuchen, N.J. and London: Scarecrow Press, 1978.

Bermant, Chaim. *London's East End: Point of Arrival*. 1975. First American Edition. New York: Macmillan, 1976.

Blackham, Robert J. *The Soul of the City: London's Livery Companies: Their Storied Past, Their Living Present*. London: Sampson, Low, Marston and Co. Ltd., n.d.

Byron, Arthur. *London Statues: A Guide to London's Outdoor Statues and Sculpture*. London: Constable, 1981.

Callen, Anthea. *Angel in the Studio: Women in the Arts and Crafts Movement, 1870–1914*. London: Astragol Books, 1979.

Crawford, Anne, et al., eds. *Europa Biographical Dictionary of British Women*. London: Europa Publications Ltd., 1983.

Dakers, Caroline. *The Blue Plaque Guide to London*. London: W.W. Norton, 1982.

Davin, Anna. *Feminist History: A Sponsored Walk*. Anna Davin, 71 Balfour Street, London.

Eagle, Dorothy and Hilary Carnell, eds. *The Oxford Literary Guide to the British Isles*. Oxford: The Clarendon Press, 1977.

East End Womens Walks. Teachers Notes; No. 2. Labour Museum, London.

Faderman, Lillian. *Surpassing the Love of Men: Romantic Friendship and Love between Women from the Renaissance to the Present*. New York: William Morrow and Co., Inc., 1981.

Fishman, William J. *Jewish Radicals: From Czarist Stetl to London Ghetto*. New York: Random House, 1974.

Fraser, Antonia. *The Weaker Vessel*. New York: Alfred A. Knopf, 1984.

Grier, Barbara and Coletta Reid, eds. *Lesbian Lives: Biographies of Women from "The Ladder."* Baltimore: Diana Press, 1976.

Holme, Thea. *Chelsea*. New York: Taplinger Publishing Co., 1971.

Lang, Elsie M. *British Women in the Twentieth Century*. London: T. Werner Laurie Ltd., 1929.

Lofts, Norah. *Queens of England*. New York: Doubleday, 1977.

Mackenzie, Midge, ed. *Shoulder to Shoulder: A Documentary*. New York: Alfred A. Knopf, 1975.

Manifold, Clare. *Feminist History in the East End*. 1979.

Morgan, Fidelis. *The Female Wits: Women Playwrights of the Restoration*. London: Virago Press, 1981.

Rose, Phyllis. *Parallel Lives: Five Victorian Marriages*. New York: Alfred A. Knopf, 1984.

Rossiter, Stuart. *London*. The Blue Guides. London: Ernest Benn Ltd., 1978.

Scobie, Edward. *Black Britannia: A History of Blacks in Britain*. Chicago: Johnson Pub. Co., Inc., 1972.

Shyllon, Folarin Olawle. *Black People in Britain, 1555–1833*. London: Oxford University Press, 1977.

Spender, Dale. *Women of Ideas and What Men Have Done To Them: From Aphra Behn to Adrienne Rich*. London: Routledge & Kegan Paul, 1982.

Taitz, Emily and Sondra Henry. *Written Out of History: Thirty centuries of Jewish Women*. New York: Bloch Publishing Co. 1978.

Uglow, Jennifer S., ed. and compiler. *International Dictionary of Women's Biography*. New York: Macmillan Publishing Co., 1982.

Weinreb, Ben and Christopher Hibbert. *The London Encyclopaedia*. London: Macmillan, 1983.

Weiser, Marjorie and Jean S. Arbeiter. *WomanList*. New York: Atheneum, 1981.

Woolf, Virginia. *The Common Reader: First Series*. New York: Harcourt, Brace and Co., Harvest, 1953.

The Second Common Reader. New York: Harcourt, Brace and Co., Harvest, 1932.

Index